AWAKEN

THE

LOVE

WITHIN

Mum, I dedicate this book to you. As a single mother you have taught me strength, loyalty, and courage. Growing up was difficult, but you filled the house with joy, love, and abundance. You are my inspiration thank you!

Thank you for the family and friends that have allowed me to grow and be able to serve the world. My brother Amrdeep Singh, you have been a massive influence of my life and shaped me to the man I am today, in many ways.

Not a day goes by without me being grateful for my grandparents moving to England, my friends, wife, and extended family for the freedom they allowed me to have during my years of becoming.

A special thanks to my wife for helping me with this book and Udhay Rehill for supporting me, push me and helping me to complete this book.

Finally, I am dedicating this book to all the single parents, singles with broken hearts, singles that didn't have the best upbringing and everyone that has not found love. I am sharing the formula that helped me find love and created love for hundreds of clients.

Thank you for purchasing this book. As part of your purchase, we are providing 1 day of access of clothing for rescued sex trafficked girls in India under your name.

Project Description

Restore the dignity of a girl rescued from commercial sexual exploitation by sponsoring clean and fresh clothing. At the time of their rescue, these girls have either minimal or no belongings.

Before being rescued they are at the mercy of their kidnappers/traffickers and are prone to physical, mental, and sexual violence. Your contribution will aid in the rehabilitation of these girls, restoring a new self-worth. Save the Children India also helps the girls to take first steps on a new path leading to a brighter future.

Contents

The number one Saboteur in relationships is 'The Stickler' is when you are seeking for perfection from an external person/ object as you have a false belief that you are perfect.

Perfect doesn't exist and if it did it will be boring!

In this book you will encounter opportunities to become the stickler, I encourage you to see the positives and take the growth needed to create the change within.

Shirzad Chamine - https://www.positiveintelligence.com

Introduction:

This book is intended to help you unleash your true lover within, using the techniques and strategies that have helped hundreds of my clients to create lasting love.

In this book, we will walk through the key things to help you understand love, create love, and heal from past problems. The steps in the books will help you become the greatest version of yourself.

I want to thank my mentors, masters, and teachers for providing me with guidance for this, and my family, who've helped me learn many things about myself and helped me grow.

I want to give a special thanks to my mum for raising me the way she did, despite the difficulties she went through. Which allowed me to learn and understand relationships and situations.

The events I went through in the past have led me to the life I live to help and to light souls up to create love.

These events led me to a path of spiritual learning, development, and personal growth. On this journey, I've encountered many outstanding people who've enabled me to grow and learn, among the most influential being Tony Robbins, who's helped me make profound shifts within my life to help me get to where I need to be.

My name is Sunny Sekhon, I am a Love Alchemist.

A love alchemist can create love from a place of anger, sadness, hurt, fear to help you become the creator of your life.

For the years, I have been helping people through healing, love, and positivity with my continued development and learning, I have been able to help clients at a deeper level.

My story started in my bedroom: alone, depressed, sad, and very isolated. It was a dark place that no fear would get me out of, where I struggled to sleep and suffered from sleep paralysis. I had no clarity because of my anxiety, pain and feared how I'd look to others. I would lose my personality trying to fit in and connect with everyone else.

I was living a life for others.

I was working in corporate finance at the time, in a job that didn't reward you for behaviour or effort, for a company that used fear to limit and control you.

To add to this, I associated myself with a negative social group, peers who would often make negative remarks, and I'd find myself losing my personality to fit in and connect with others.

I took on pain, suffering, and worry as an unaware empath. I was constantly absorbing any negativity around me. I wouldn't know how to let go of that feeling within. It led me into even more darkness, making me criticize and disrespect myself. I couldn't recognize who I was!

I drifted into a negative thinking pattern, in which I constantly doubted myself. I lost my inner confidence and was afraid to speak up and express who I was.

Then there was one night where I thought to myself, 'this isn't how I want my life to remain; this isn't what I want anymore.'

My environment wasn't serving me and was causing me to suffer. I was working in a job I didn't like. I was starting a relationship with someone I genuinely connected with, but the people close to me were against it - this was all leading to my world to collapsing.

My family turned on me because I formed a relationship. The closest people in my world, my brother, and my mother, whom I loved dearly. They misunderstood the situation regarding my partner.

They were scared and made negative assumptions because they thought they would lose me; they thought if I was in a relationship, I would leave them.

These events led me into a state of depression and pain and self-discovery since I had nowhere else to turn. The external world wasn't serving me anymore, and I was in a relationship with somebody I loved.

I had to turn within.

I wasn't in a good place.

I felt limited, consumed by negative emotions, and lost!

When I started my journey, the only place to look for answers was within. That's when life changed for me in an impactful way.

Let's quickly talk about how my life changed for me!

I'm married in a passionate, loving, beautiful relationship. I run a successful business where I help people create love in their lives -something that I love - and help to serve and give back. I'm the leader and the creator of my life. I've been on many great holidays, I've travelled, I've seen many great places and experienced a beautiful degree of energy.

My relationship with my family is terrific.

I live with a high level of joy and gratitude in my life. Most importantly, I am the person I am for me and not for someone else. I'm not here to please and to get validation from others. When I started this journey of personal development and learning, I learned so much about myself on a conscious and subconscious level.

I will be sharing some of the things that genuinely changed my life, from being single and unhappy to entering a healthy relationship filled with love and passion.

My journey started when I first attended a Tony Robbins event! It began with me looking deeply within myself and finding out who I truly am.

I hid my deeper problems and covered them by blaming the outside world for many years. I'm still searching for who I truly am, but I know myself much better than when I first started my journey.

The most profound shift that occurred to me from learning from Tony Robbins was that I began to understand how to master myself, manage my emotions, and take the lead of my life.

I'm grateful for having this mentor in my life, as he's helped me grow and expand significantly from who I was and created an opening for me in coaching. Soon after, I became a qualified coach, specifically in life coaching. I qualified in NLP as a practitioner, timeline therapy, RTT hypnosis, and in many other areas. Hypnosis allowed me to help clients delve deep into their subconscious thoughts and beliefs, rewiring their minds to help them achieve tremendous success.

I started with coaching married couples and had great success; I was known for my re-marriage package, which helped my clients rebuild their foundations of a relationship, taking accountability and committing to a higher level of relationship.

I then studied singles behaviours and learnt the keys aspects that were missing and was able to develop strategies to help them find lasting love with the right foundations.

Now it's time for you to shine and build the relationship you deserve.

This book will talk through the guiding principles that have helped hundreds of my clients create love in their lives.

I'm going to share breakthroughs from my clients that I've coached through their journeys to give different perspectives of different relationships, which required different solutions so you can determine which is most applicable for you.

A few years ago, I came across a beautiful book, Your Soul's Plan, by Robert Schwartz. The book had a massive impact on my life, and after further research into Robert's work, it resonated with my soul and allowed me to let go of any hidden, lingering pains and have since used his expertise to help clients.

Your soul's plan has a distinct idea that we plan our existence on Earth and the challenges we face to learn lessons to develop the soul. We set up the events and people around us to help us understand and become greater versions of ourselves.

Your soul's plan helps us to understand that every experience in life is a lesson to be learned, to allow us to grow to a higher level.

When I first understood this, it helped me accept a lot of the pain in my life as I began to view it from a different perspective; it helped me let go of the anger I was holding on to. As I took responsibility for planning the painful experiences I encountered in life.

Imagine if all the past events in your life were only intended to help you grow?

We will be expanding on this notion during the later chapters of this book.

The secret to healing is knowing that there is a greater plan, and your experience shape you to become more.

Be open and ready for this transformative process.

Chapter 1:

Finding self-love

Welcome to the start of this transformative book.

The next level of your love life is waiting on the other side of these papers.

All great things start with self-love!

Without self-love, life will be daunting and will limit our growth. Self-love is why we have energy, and self-love is why we get out of bed.

This book will help you uncover the keys to creating the profound, lasting relationship you want.

Before we move on to the other areas, we must be confident that you have the proper habits in place to build your confidence, self-love, joy, and happiness.

These are the critical areas for myself and my clients who've been able to transform their level of love in their life.

I invite you to commit to this love journey and to begin implementing the learning as quickly as possible.

One of the critical areas of life is to have a deep level of self-love. If we miss these simple practices, it could be the difference between you being in deep loving relationship or staying single!

Following this system has helped many of my clients to be able to maintain who they are, become more balanced and centred within.

So, for us to start showing up as more in the world, let's start by creating more inner love habits.

Task: Fill out the wheel and base it on seven days of the week.

How many days are you meeting your goals?

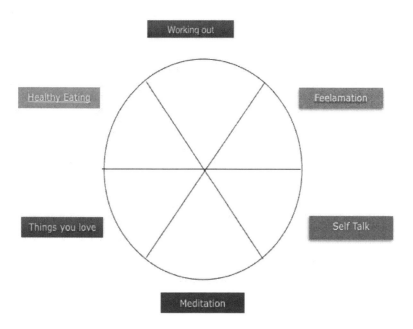

I have created an amazing Facebook group that will keep you accountable for your self-love throughout this process. For the next 28 days, I would like you to create these habits and be responsible with other bachelors in the group.

(Who knows, who you may meet!)

https://linktr.ee/sunnysekhon

1) Healthy eating: How often are you eating right now?

What we put into our bodies is what we become - for example, if we put junk and unhealthy foods into our bodies, we start feeling low. What changes can you make today to help raise your vibration?

Fewer takeaways, alcohol, sugars? Healthier food, lighter meals.

When we feel low, we do not feel like dating and connecting with the world. We do not feel like shining our light. Eating healthy is one of the most essential things for boosting our inner confidence, and thus increasing self-love.

When you take care of your body, you are showing your self-love. How well are you currently eating, and what is your target?

Are you eating good foods? Alright, write that down and be honest with yourself.

Are you happy with that number?

If not, how would you like to increase it?

Would you like to eat better (more salads, fewer drinks, less meat?)

Five times a week, I am happy to do intermittent fasting, which has fantastic benefits for overall health and discipline. Studies have also found that you will see long-term benefits when you do a five to two ratio of fasting.

(Healthline) 10 Evidence-Based Health Benefits of Intermittent Fasting

Intermittent fasting is an eating pattern where you cycle between periods of eating and fasting.

There are many different types of intermittent fasting, such as the 16/8 and 5:2 methods.

Numerous studies show that it can have powerful benefits for your body and brain.

Here are 10 evidence-based health benefits of intermittent fasting.

Changes the function of hormones, cells, and genes

Can help you lose weight and visceral fat

Can reduce insulin resistance, lowering your risk for type 2 diabetes

Can reduce oxidative stress and inflammation in the body

It May be beneficial for heart health.

Induces various cellular repair processes

It May help prevent cancer

Has benefits for your brain

It May help prevent Alzheimer's disease

May extend your lifespan

Intermittent fasting has changed my life; It's helped me develop my inner game, it's helped me become cautious of my thoughts, feelings, and awareness because when we limit the amount of food that can enter our body, it puts our minds into a state of survival, and we start to worry. The more we can manage that feeling, the better we become at reducing stress dealing with life's obstacles.

In addition, a great natural supplement I use is called KaliCha Shilajit.

The benefits are excellent; it helps with clarity, nutrition, weight loss, and balancing hormones for males and females. This means better testosterone in men and women means more regular cycles.

This hidden gem is from India and is a natural substance from the Himalayan mountains. Here is a link to www.kalicha.com for this product as it is essential to get a pure resin substance.

There are a lot of studies that show the power of this substance, and it has been medically tested, showing excellent benefits; the most common use of it is for the overall energy and sexual organ regeneration.

2) Working out?

How often are you working out, and is your body where you want it to be?

Be honest with yourself!

How often, for how long? Do you need to be doing more?

If it is twice a week, what's the intensity of the workouts?

Can you put in an extra day or go for a walk?

Can you add in a weight session?

Can you add in an extra yoga session?

Most people get put off working out because of having high expectations over a short period. Working out is like everything else. Consistency makes the long-term difference; if you do something once, it won't change who you are, but it will impact you if you turn it into a habit.

Your whole-body shape can change; making little steps will increase your confidence, help you feel more complete, and create the outer image you deserve whilst working on the inner game.

Think about all the things you will be able to do with more energy; imagine being able to run across the beach with your partner or future children.

How would that feel?

Let's declare it now!

How often are you going to work out?
What days?
How long?

Also, what is a theme song that can get you excited to train?

Science shows there is a strong link between music and the state that you feel.

Is there a powerful song that can help you get into the mood of working out?

3) *Meditation is being able to access heaven on Earth.*

"With meditation, you become a sensitized superhero, completely in control, with endless possibilities at your fingertips."
— Tara Stiles

I've learned this technique through the years I've spent meditating every day - it has helped me tremendously in achieving peace with myself.

It also increased my ability to remain calm during stressful times.

You can meditate anywhere; it is a state of mind that can be switched on and off - you can command the body how you want to feel in the given moment. Centering ourselves is the critical part of creating a passionate relationship.

I highly recommend a 5-minute meditation every day to help you take charge of your emotions. It is important because it allows you to take control of the emotions you want to experience throughout the day.

If you wake up feeling frustrated, you will experience a frustrating day. If you wake up feeling joy, you will handle stressful obstacles much easier.

Meditating tells the body how it wants to feel on that day and then steps into that feeling.

"And can you teach your body emotionally
what it would feel like to believe in this way

to be empowered . . .
to be moved by your greatness . . .
to be invincible . . .
to have courage . . .
to be in love with life . . .
to feel unlimited . . .
to live as if your prayers are already
answered?. ."

Joe Dispenza

Many people claim that they don't have the time to
meditate. Well, the truth is, it creates more time.

Joe Dispenza, You Are the Placebo: Making Your Mind Matter

4) The next area I want to cover is what you love to do?

I would like you to create a habit of doing the things that you love:

Working out,
Reading,
Going for walks
Listening to music,
Cooking.

Whatever it is, I would like you to make a list of the things you love and start to implement them in your life.

How can we attract love when we don't love the life we already live?

As simple as this sounds, it could be a game-changer in your life.

There was a time I was struggling to work and focus. It was taking all the joy out of my life and drained my energy; eventually, I got burnt out.

Then, I took up a new sport.

I took up tennis and fell in love with it. The amount of strategy and focus required appealed to me. It helped me shift from a state of being stuck to a state of passion. I applied this energy to other areas of my life and eventually got my flow back.

Now, I'd like you to think of something you love and implement that into your daily habits.

5) The next area is your self-talk!

Most of us are very critical and hard on ourselves, which can sometimes work in our favour, such as when we know we can work harder at something. However, within relationships, this will have a negative impact if we are consistently putting ourselves down. A relationship reflects how you treat yourself, and the more disrespectfully you treat yourself, the more you will project those emotions onto your partner.

By telling yourself:

I am stupid
I am not good enough
I will never be able to achieve it.

Why would anyone love you? This attitude will push away love. Imagine talking to your best friend like that - would you have many friends in your life?

Imagine how your life would be if you started to tell yourself.

I am a genius.
I can do this.

I am an inspiration; how would you appear if you held these inner beliefs?

As such, next time a negative thought enters your mind, I'd like you to replace it with the positive opposite.

Bad thoughts:

'I'm bad at this'
'There's nothing special about me'

Good thoughts:

'I am learning to be the best.'
'I am unique.'

I know the survival part of your brain is saying, 'I need to pressure you to be better,' but how has that served you up until now?

It's time to tap into the part of you that is thriving.

That is the creator of life, bringing out the best parts of you.

Therefore, I'm encouraging you to start telling yourself something you love about yourself when you wake up.

Start by making a gratitude list of who you are, how you are, and the things that you are grateful for in life?

I am a caring person
I am a funny
I am the light
I love my resilience

Being grateful for the smallest way that you show up to the world is a blessing.

I will leave lines below for you to start filling out your daily gratitude list.

_____

_____

_____

_____

_____

_____

_____

_____

_____

_____

_____

_____

_____

_____

_____

_____

_____

_____

_____

_____

_____

_____

_____

_____

_____

_____

_____

_____

_____

_____

_____

_____

You can come back to this whenever you are not feeling your best.

Next is Feelamation:

Feelamation is feeling the words that are spoken, feeling the vibration of the words you are saying, feeling it internally to every cell in your body.

A Feelamation is not like an affirmation. Affirmations are spoken words of encouragement, but while the positive thinking is there, assertions may fail you as a transformative technique. You can recite something uplifting, but if you aren't embodying it physically, you are only skimming the surface.

I am love

You will feel the loving energy within you by thinking of someone that you love and linking that feeling of love to every time you say I am love.

"Be careful of your moods and feelings, for there is an unbroken connection between your feelings and your visible world. Your body is an emotional filter and bears the unmistakable marks of your prevalent emotions."

— Neville Goddard, Feeling is the Secret

Feelings are the key to creating the environment you live in; when you feel a negative state, you will attract more negativity around you. Therefore, by changing your feeling, you will change the external world.

You are the command you tell yourself when you connect with the feeling.

I am love.
I am attracting love into my life.

I am more than enough.
The universe is bringing the right people into my life.
I am grateful for all the obstacles in my life.
I have excellent relationships in my life.

Task:
I would like you to post in the Facebook group your results and commitment to how you will show up in the world.

https://linktr.ee/sunnysekhon

How you do anything is how you do everything!

The way you show up in
life on a day-to-day basis,
is a direct reflection how your
relationships will be!

Chapter 2:

Attachment styles

Your attachment style controls your behaviours within relationships

My partner and I would argue all the time due to the differences in our attachment styles. We were both anxious within the relationship, which meant we needed reassurance constantly. If we did not receive it, we wouldn't feel love.

It led us down a path of destructive behaviours and vicious arguments for many years, and we were treading on eggshells to maintain the relationship.

When we discovered what was causing the neediness and the issues within the relationship, we resolved it and have been able to create a beautiful relationship. We discovered our sabotaging factors from out attachment styles and noticed when we were acting up due to our upbringing. Once we healed the past, we healed the relationship. Therefore, understanding your attachment style is crucial to developing a deeper connection.

Attachment styles are formed from the first seven years of life. Psychological studies have shown that how attentive and loving parents are towards their children can significantly impact the child's relationship journey.

The basis of my work comes from understanding how we form relationships and the different attachment styles that impact our relationship decisions.

Attachments develop in early childhood, based on our caregiver's affection to the child. Psychology studies have shown this to affect future relationship behaviours, which can be either Secure, anxious, scared or Avoidant with accompanying Negative Self-Regard Tendency (NST).

For children, their early years consist of intense emotional experiences. The parent's parenting style shapes the type of adult that child will become, it affects how much they trust, open and how they feel in relationships.

Thye safer the child can feel growing up, will determine how safe they feel connecting with others. The secure attachment style makes them feel safe, loved, and empowered to take risks and open.

Love is a leap of faith, which may prove to be an incredible risk, but also a great reward if you are ready to find someone who loves you too. Using the strategies in this book it will allow you to be ready for a relationship and to open your heart!

If your business goes down, you understand why sales are down, or customers are asking for refunds, you can change the strategy and try a new approach to build a business.

Relationships are different; if the connection dies, so does a part of you, and it's hard for you to understand the detail of why especially when you open your heart.

It's not like you're opening a bank account; your heart is such a sacred, blessed place of deep intermit connection. By understanding relationships and love at a deeper level, it allows us to prepare and be ready to create love.

Attachment styles are a profound tool to understand human behaviours and relationship behaviour to reduce the fear of love.

A person's attachment style would have an internal formula programmed in the subconscious mind. A hurt formula will look like **'love equals pain'** a secure formula will be **'love equals joy'** and needy mind will play a formula that **'love equals attention'**.

The brain's job is straightforward: ***it moves us away from pain and moves us towards pleasure.***

Therefore, our subconscious mind mainly dominates the area of relationships, and this interferes when we consciously want to form a relationship. That is why we continuously attract the wrong partner without being aware or similarly pushing relationships away after a certain period.

When you are in love, you may experience a spectacular feeling of excitement, joy, euphoria, an unbeatable feeling of being on top of the world. Love is one of these things you predominantly feel, and it isn't easy to measure. This is because love is connected to your heart, not your mind.

Our emotions are linked to our subconscious and our higher level of thinking. Therefore, it's difficult for us to truly love without dealing with the attachment styles that have already been planted from childhood.

Now that we understand how our attachment styles affect our relationships, we will now detail the various attachment styles and understand how this impacts the relationships you create.

The 4 main attachment styles:

The secure attachment style:

The first is the secure attachment style. A secure attachment style refers to when we can live freely, free of any hurt, sense of abandonment, or feelings that we are unloved. Those who adopt this style, have grown up with independence and awareness that there is and has always been somebody there when needed.

A child's ability to form an early sense of security is crucial for their future development. This sense of security is largely determined by the amount of support and unconditional love they receive from their parents.

When love and support are given in abundance, it enables children to understand that there will be someone to provide support despite any of the circumstances they may encounter within their life.

The avoidant attachment style:

Contrary to those of the secure attachment style, people who are avoidants were often hurt or abandoned as children and may not seek close relationships out of fear that it will cause the pain to return, even though they crave love just like everyone else does!

This is a strong pattern for me whilst growing up, I would be scared that the relationship wouldn't work which led me to sabotaging them by not committing to my partner and talking to multiple people at once. I was trying to protect myself from being hurt by one person.

When we adopt an avoidant attachment style, we build a defence mechanism that says: "I will never love again because I don't want to be hurt again." The consequence of doing this is you put a guard up and don't let people in, 'I don't want anyone to hurt me in this way, or to bring me down.

The avoidant attachment style becomes very closed-off to love, they become very logical, measured, and is typically very successful in their work. Due to the certainty and significance that work will give them, allowing them to create results with less chances of being hurt.

These formulas generally consist of:

More work output equals better results and love equals pain.

The anxious attachment style:

The anxious attachment style is known for being the needy, the clingy, the co-dependent type. This attachment style is formed because the child never received as much love or attention growing up, forcing them to crave attention to receive love.

Those who adopt the anxious attachment style carry the belief that they must receive attention and try to hold on to it. This way, they'll receive the attention they needed when growing up, through such methods as fussing or exaggerating situations.

Therefore, they have an equation that says love equals attention in their mind. As a result of this, they can't differentiate between love and attention and will often force the attention of somebody in a good or bad way to get the love they seek.

An example of this occurring would be when a child falls ill and receives additional love and support. When this continually occurs, the child begins to feign sickness, to receive greater attention, as they become aware that it will lead to greater love.

The scared attachment style is:

The scared attachment style comprises of worry and self-blame, which are frequently derived from childhood neglect. These individuals develop a habit of blaming themselves for the pain they've experienced, despite it being caused by a lack of love from their parents.

Those with this attachment style often carry a victim mentality: they'll view themselves as victims of relationships and love and will hold the perspective that they cannot enter a relationship because they're "just not good enough." In addition, they'll feel as though if they try to be open and honest, they'll be attacked and humiliated.

This feeling is supposed to serve the purpose of protecting them from being hurt. The state of mind and attachment style prevents people from reaping the rewards of the world, whether it be in terms of life or relationships.

In later chapters, I will provide guidance on shifting from these negative attachment styles to that of secure.

Why is being secure or having a partner that is secure important?

As previously stated, an individual with a secure attachment style lives freely, without any emotional pain.

To refer to the question, having this is vital because 70% of individuals who carry a secure attachment style are in long-term relationships or married after the age of 35. In addition, based on a statistic produced in 2018, those who are avoidant or anxious - traits that contradict that of the secure attachment style - are more likely to encounter divorce.

Understanding this gives us great insight and power to transform your love destiny and will allow you to create more profound love. Over these following few chapters, we're going to be diving deeper into your identity, allowing you to let go of any deep unmet needs from your childhood.

It's time to let go of the story that holds you back. We will now rewrite the parts of your life that don't serve you anymore to allow you to become the best version of yourself.

'You must divorce your old story and marry your new story.'

Your past story has gotten you to where you are right now. It's now time to divorce that story and merge it into a new one, to get you to where you want to be.

Divorcing the story of the past allows us to let go of the pain, suffering, and the negative beliefs that we hold onto from the past to allow us to find a new story, a new pathway for the future.

What do I mean by divorcing the story?

Divorcing your stories is letting go of your subconscious blocks.

When blaming others from the negative experiences that shows up in life, it is essential to rise above the situation and to consciously blame seeing the positives and the negatives.

My story before was one of aggression. I used to argue and fight a lot when I was younger, and this all happened because I used to blame many people in my life. I blamed my father for physically abusing my mother, and by blaming him, it gave me comfort and reinforced my anger and perspective of my life. I chose to hold my anger within and would reflect a cheerful and joyous facade. On the inside, I was angry and upset.

During my younger years, this created a lot of trouble, and my defensive behaviour will always find me in arguments and disagreements. I was holding on to a story of pain which create pain in my life.

My father physically abused my mum, hurting her and causing misery and pain to her, it led to my mother having mental health conditions, and I helped her from a young age to help raise her and help support her through the hardest of times.

I used only to think, 'if I had a father that was there for me, that could support me, life would be much better. Why did he do this to us?'

Therefore, I couldn't develop the deeper relationships that I wanted my life. This was the pain that came up in my life.

That was my old story.

Task: Now, I would like you to write down a story of your own. A story from when you were young if you never received the love you wanted from your family. A story of an unhealthy childhood or relationship.

Any of the stories that serve only to undermine your relationship journey.

Whatever first comes to mind, I would like you to write it now.

It is essential that you take part in these exercises to break through and achieve the outcome that you want to get to the level of life that you seek.

_____

_____

_____

_____

_____

From understanding all the negatives that I blamed my father for, it is time to consciously blame for the positives.

I must thank my father for being the way he is because this has helped me become a more caring, loving person who understands people and truly cares about the world and the happiness of others. The suffering I witnessed helped shape me to understand people and make powerful decisions in life to stop suffering in the world.

I am now a compassionate, caring man that will never hurt women. I thank him as he helped me choose this mission in life to empower other souls and help them find love.

He is the reason I'm writing this book. He is the reason I care so much. I thank him for making me want to help millions of lives. I thank him for making me want to stop human sex trafficking within the world.

I thank him for making me the man I am today.
This all helped me become this person that I am caring, loving and strive to be the best version of myself.

If it wasn't for my father, if it wasn't for the struggles I experienced during my childhood, I would not be the person I am today. I would never have been this caring, I would never have set my goal to help millions of people, and I would have been working in corporate finance still.

What is your new story?

Who have you become because of the past? How has it made you more robust, caring, loving, and compassionate?

I'm going to introduce you to three characters that I've personally worked with, and for client confidentiality, I have changed their names.

Meet Aron; he is a very successful man who works very hard with his own business. He has an avoidant attachment style because his father abandoned him from a young age. This has a massive impact on his success in long-term relationships; he can date for long periods. However, when the connection is ready to go to the next level, he usually finds something to move away from them.

'She is not the one.'

'She wouldn't fit in with my family.'

He has come to me for support because he is not finding the relationship he desperately wants. Whenever it is time for commitment, he will run away. Therefore, he came to me to open his mind and help him form a deeper relationship.

Meet Sharon; Sharon is a single mom that has had some bad relationships in the past. And these bad relationships have made her not want to open and connect again. Sharon was sexually abused from a young age, and because of that, she's been scared and has a negative meaning towards love. She has formed an anxious, scared attachment style, where she gives too much. She has become a pleaser in relationships.

She lives beyond her needs and loses herself in relationships.

In the next few chapters, we will understand Sharon's story more.

Meet Jade; Jade is a secure attachment style. She has had an excellent upbringing, her parents loved her deeply, and she understood and saw the beautiful relationship as growing up.

When Aron first understood this concept of the story. Aron had a lot of blame and resentment for his father hidden away; he covered it up by saying, I am not annoyed at him. I forgot about him, and it didn't impact my life. This is a normal reaction as he knows thinking about the situation does not serve him or his business, but he is an avoidant because he avoids complex topics.

When we did the exercise of blaming for the problem, he had a similar breakthrough to my own, where he blamed his father, hurting him, leaving him, and causing problems to his family. Then he realized that the issues he caused helped him become a successful businessman that helped him grow, helped him overcome problems and become independent, and helped him travel the world and be more of who he is. If it weren't for that, he wouldn't be able to express and be the creator of his life.

This exercise was too painful for Sharon because there was a lot of blame and hurt inside her.

Sharon took all the responsibility for the problems in her life, even the issues of others.

Sharon's story that she had to divorce was a father abusing her sexually, afraid of sexual abuse. It caused her bad relationships; it caused her problems with trust and feeling unsafe.

(Side note: I truly respect Sharon for how she has been able to change her view on this event. Sexual abuse is terrible, and I am sickened by how common it is in the world and the lack of awareness it gets. There is an opportunity to grow, build resilience and be stronger in this life.)

Due to her past, it limited Sharon as it was difficult for her to love and to open her heart, it created self-worth issues, and she would be mistreated in relationships a lot. She needed to divorce the story that she was not good enough, that she's not lovable, that people could treat her the way they were treating her.

She blamed her father for the cost of her marriage, her insecurities, her fear every night before she went to bed. She blamed him for negatively seeing the world. She blamed him for accusing all the people she met of cheating on her and not wanting to be with her.

When she blamed the good that came from the past, she realized that there was a gift in the problem. She realized that because her father sexually abused her. She is now caring, loving, kind, and considerate to the world. She would do anything not to hurt another person.

It taught her to stand up for herself and be more robust; she showed that she could get through anything. It helped her become more of the light. She knew that she could be the light even when darkness was out there in the world. She learned that she could be more than anything happening around her, no matter the situation.

It allowed her to connect to the people and help others struggling; she realized that this helped build her into a better person adding light to the world.

Jade looked at this; she understood that her story wasn't related to childhood trauma. It was her perception of the world because she believed it was perfect.

Jade's old story thought that men were evil. In her previous relationship, Jade was cheated on, making her doubt herself and not believe in men. She started to think she wasn't good enough and being her wasn't enough.

(Side note: I find cheating as a cowardice act, when you can not discuss your differences in a relationship or end the relationship means you are not living in courage. I know this because I have cheated in the past and that was the vibration I was living in; I didn't have courage to communicate if I wasn't happy with the relationship. Thankfully I have developed that part of me.)

She had to divorce her story, that she's not worthy, and people will cheat on her, and the natural world is different from her upbringing. She had to divorce the story. The other people are better than her because her body is not pleasant. She isn't as attractive as others.

Looking at all the pains that she went through, other troubles that she had because of relationships, and the pain it brought in. It changed her approach to thinking about love, how people are up, and how she can't be as secure as she would like.

The new story was knowing all the positives that came from that cheat now; she knows what she wants within a relationship. She is now able to tell the signs of disrespectful behaviour within relationships.

She knows not to be naive in relationships and life. She also saw it as a gift that they cheated this early; what if he cheated again in the future, perhaps when they have children.

This experience helped her understand people more and have more emotional intelligence. It taught her to be more of a leader within life and relationships, leading her to trust her intuition more.

It taught her not to settle and know what she will tolerate within relationships.

Attached: The New Science of Adult Attachment and How It Can Help You Find--and Keep—Love - Book by Amir Levine and Rachel S. F. Heller

Chapter 3:

'Forgiveness is the gateway to peace'

The act of forgiveness is the most significant gift to yourself. Most people believe that forgiveness is to let someone off the hook. Well, forgiving is the most beautiful gift you can give yourself.

The Tennen & Affleck studies support that forgiveness helps overall health and mental well-being. It increases positive emotions while reducing negative ones, such as blame and anger, benefits our cardiovascular health and reduces ill health.

(Tennen & Affleck, 1990; Miller, Smith, Turner, Guijarro, & Hallet, 1996

How forgiveness changed my life!

I was always an angry person; I held on too many things. There was a lot of stress with my family, my father, and the people around me.

When I was holding on to the past, I thought it was good because I thought I was hurting them for their wrongdoing at a deeper level. However, the only hurting person was me as I held on to pain and hurt from the past.

The first time someone asked me to forgive, I thought, why must I forgive them? They did me wrong. Why should I let them off the hook? I felt that they should be asking for my forgiveness, and it triggered me, I was annoyed at the thought of forgiving them.

That's when I realized I was holding on to the pain still, it wasn't about forgiving them; I was letting go of the pain I held in my subconscious mind for a long time.

They still have to live with what they did, and some call it Karma; some call it the mirror of the mind. When someone has wronged somebody, there will be a mirrored reflection in their world that will attract the same people into their lives and cause the same issues.

We forgive and learn the lessons.

When we forget and do not learn from the lesson, the pattern will repeat, but when we know and understand more about the person, we can let go of the pain as we have learned our lesson.

We're letting go of the pain, the suffering, the hurt for us to be able to live a free life and to be happy. Being happy is the ideal place for many people.

Many studies have shown that forgiveness helps us with energy, creative flow, and happiness. Forgiveness is one of the keys to helping us raise our consciousness.

Like attracts like, therefore, when we are holding onto past pains and problems, even though we are consciously not thinking of the problem, we still haven't forgiven the person or situation. Therefore, we will attract more people of the same nature.

Holding on to issues is a tiring experience, even when we attempt to numb the pain with distractions such as alcohol or gossip. When holding onto resentment, we use force to get by in life and find arguments in many situations to be correct because we do not want to be hurt again.

It depletes your energy.

It starts taking away from your greatness.

Knowing this makes me choose forgiveness.

'Hurt people hurt people'

By understanding this belief, I know that the person annoyed and swearing at another are hurting deep down, which is why they behave this way.

I was hoping you could think about that for a moment.

Hurt people hurt people.

That means that people are suffering and not in their best state, which is why they start to hurt other people.

Task: I would like you to write down on your piece of paper what's the worst thing that you have done to someone? Have you shouted at somebody aggressively?

Have you been accused of things that are not true?

Have you cheated on someone?

Have you thought evil thoughts about someone?

We both know that it was not how you wanted to handle the situation; you were under stress, and that's why you acted differently.

Trust your unconscious mind. Write down the first thing or the second worst thing you have done in the past.

The key to this is accepting that we all do bad things, and it isn't because you are a terrible person, but you were in a bad emotional energy at the time.

The secret healing technique

I'm going to introduce you to a magnificent unique forgiveness process taught by Dr Joe Vitale.

This forgiveness technique is called the Ho'oponopono.

I know it's a tongue twister.

The ho'oponopono first came about in Hawaii by a doctor called Dr Len. He used this powerful forgiveness technique to help thousands of families and people let go and move forward from health problems, stress, and relationship issues.

This forgiveness technique can energetically free any of the blocks we have and any pains because it allows us to be accountable for what happened and let go.

The foundation of this practice is unity: an unbreakable bond connects you to everyone else, even though we seem separate.

When errors are corrected externally, errors are corrected internally. When you "cleanse" your consciousness, you contribute to cleansing the "collective consciousness." When you forgive others, you are also purified.

There is a legendary story of a man known as Dr Ihaleakala Hew Len, who cured every patient in the criminally insane ward of a Hawaii State Hospital — without ever seeing a single patient. Now, this may seem a little "insane," but upon having a closer look, the story speaks for itself.

Dr Len set up an office to review his patients' files.

The patients at the hospital pleaded insanely at court. They were convicts, murderers, rapists, killers, the worst of the worst. No doctors or nurses wanted to work there or be a part of it. They would be so scared that they would walk with their backs against the wall. The patients were on the strongest medications and minimum free time because of the violence in the institution.

Dr Len said I don't need to see these patients to heal them. I can recover them from a distance. I'll help them and free the blocks they have within.

Dr Len would look through the patient records, see what they were in for, and take responsibility for what they did.

He said it was my responsibility for what they did. He would look at their photos and read their profiles. He would take on what they did and then do forgiveness for them and clear the energy.

Forgiveness is very simple.

The first step: Accountability: Somehow, it was my fault; I must take accountability for what happened.

Then the power lines are:

I'm sorry

Please forgive me

Thank you

I love you

I'm sorry for repenting anything that has happened. It is in our mind, which means it is part of our life. Repenting for it will allow us to free the energy.

Please forgive me for asking for forgiveness. Don't worry about who you're asking. Just ask! PLEASE FORGIVE ME. Say it over and over. Mean it. We have all had a time when we have done wrong, so forgiveness is at a deeper level.

Gratitude: Say "THANK YOU" – again, and it doesn't matter who or what you're thanking. Thank your body for all it does for you. Thank yourself for being the best you can be. Thank God. Thank the Universe. Thank whatever it was that just forgave you. Just keep saying THANK YOU.

Love – I LOVE YOU moving forward beautifully and allowing them to see who you are.

Dr Len continued to repeat this and feel the forgiveness happening. It's amazing what happened after that.

After three months of medication within the asylum, the violence reduced.

After six months, inmates returned, saying they wanted to go to prison and pay the price for my crime. Many inmates are completing their time in jail and have been released for good behaviour.

After 18 months, the asylum has become a powerful ritual of forgiveness.

It's one that my wife and I use after an argument. In the past, we would hold on to the issues for a long time; however, now, we will let it go by using this process, and then we would say it and laugh and let go of any of the problems.

Task: I would like you to think of someone you need to forgive and write down their name and what you need to forgive.

Close your eye and imagine them in front of you.

As you do, let's forgive them.

And if you're driving, please save this for later.

Close your eyes.

Take three deep breaths and get centred within yourself.

Thank you for your attention.

Now say

I'm sorry

Please forgive me

Thank you

I love you

Three times

Imagine them smiling and sending love back to you.

Now, take a deep breath in and out, releasing any energy that's not wanted.

Link to meditation:
https://www.youtube.com/watch?v=wvT8Ffy83s0&t=18s

One of my clients used this method, to forgive her sister, they hadn't spoken for 12 years due to an argument that they had. After using this practice for a few weeks her sister contacted her out of the blue.

Here's how my clients have been able to use this. They would think of someone that deeply hurt them and followed this method of forgiveness.

Aron had to get clear of all the people who have hurt him in the past and the people he had hurt; he had to understand what he had done to make people feel bad, cry, or put them down. He remembered a particular situation in which he argued with his brother.

He had been disrespectful, and Aron got mad and said many evil things; since then, they haven't spoken the way they used to. His brother was his best friend in the past, but they hadn't spoken based on the argument.

Aron learned to take accountability for the situation and began to do the Ho'oponopono to let go of any tension between them. He started to see it from his brother's point of view and truly forgave the situation instantly. Aron felt better about things, and a few weeks later, his brother messaged in which they both started to rebuild their relationship.

I know many of you are thinking about how a problem with your brother would affect your love life. Once we feel like we are not complete, we put different energy into relationships, and part of us will feel incomplete.

How Aron completed this exercise:

1) He closed his eyes, imagined what happened in the argument, and returned to that time.

2) He saw the argument from his side of things.
He was annoyed and frustrated that his brother never took responsibility and was disrespectful.

3) He then saw it from his brother's point of view.
His brother was going through stress and was in the wrong financial place, making him think he was not good enough.

4) Aron then saw the argument through a bird's eye view watching above it.

From the birds-eye perspective, he saw that it was a misunderstanding and not personal that they had both not been in the best state.

Now Aron visualized looking at his brother and doing the Ho'oponopono forgiveness until he felt better.

I'm sorry.
Please forgive me.
I love you.
Thank you.

The three levels of forgiveness.

The first level is self-forgiveness. Many people think, why must I forgive myself?

Well, we all know at some level that we could have handled the situation differently, or sometimes we have been too hard on ourselves.

Forgiving ourselves helps us to let go of anything holding us back.

The second level of forgiveness is for others, which could be for anything, such as a situation where we feel like we have been wronged or hurt.

We need to understand that the other person is also human, and they are doing the best that they can at that moment, which might not be good enough for us, but it's good enough for them.

The third level is universal forgiveness, and this is where we can let go of anything that we have been holding on to anger, resentment, pain, etc.

Forgiveness could be towards people, situations, or even towards God.

Trusting that life is happening for a greater purpose, even the argument or fights you had could have been the best lesson for another person.

'Life happens for us not to us'- Tony Robbins.

Trusting everything happens for a reason allows significant opportunities for growth. Realizing this is the start of the alchemy process.

Sharon uses this technique to free herself from the nightmares and suffering she has taken on throughout her life.

Sharon had many blocks in life linked to the energy that she felt inside; she was sexually abused from a young age and thought that it was her fault this happened to her.

Sharon had resistance forgiving the family that abused her as she was holding on to the past for so long that it was uncomfortable to let it go.

Sharon would be angry towards others and internally because she consciously knew what others did to her was wrong, but subconsciously, she held on to shame that made her think it was her fault.

It was her fault that she never spoke up about the situation and her fault that she wasn't strong enough.

It was a challenging process for Sharon; she knew that she needed to heal the past wounds for her happiness and find the right partner.
She said to me, 'Do you expect me to let him off the hook with what he has done to me?'

I replied, 'We are not letting anyone off the hook, he will get what is meant to happen to him, and he will create the life of pain due to the way he is.'

I asked, 'How much more time in your mind do you want to give him?'

Sharon replied, 'No more, I have thought of him too much, he has been in my mind for the last 40 years, and it has caused me deep pain.'

I replied, 'Let's move on with your life now.'

We began the process of forgiveness.

Sharon's first person to forgive was herself for allowing herself to feel guilty and ashamed of the event. Forgive herself for the times that she thought it was her fault.

She imagined looking at the younger version of herself, and she spoke to herself and said;

'I'm sorry: for taking on the responsibility and shame.'

Please forgive me: for all the evenings that I was abusing myself with bad words, alcohol, and allowing others to treat me this way.

I love you: for being strong and overcoming all the obstacles in life. I love you for being brave. I love you for smiling every day and giving joy to others.

Thank you: thank you for accepting my forgiveness and for moving on.

She repeated this process a few times to free the uncomfortable feeling.

Now she got into a comfortable position, and I asked her to go back to an argument or situation with her father. She saw it from his point of view, of what he was going through (even as difficult as it might sound).

She looked at the situation through his eye and saw that this man felt that no one loved him, he had no respect for himself, and others mistreated him; he was a hurt man.

And even though he had no right to do this to her, she saw how broken he was, which helped her understand his side.

She then imagined him in front of her and went through the Forgiveness process.

I'm sorry

Please forgive me

I love you

Thank you

She is handing this pain over to God, infinite intelligence, to let it go from her life. When Sharon completed this process, she felt lighter and free from pain.

Now it's time for you to do this. I have created a meditation for you to complete online when you are in a safe place, relaxed, and settling down for the evening.

Chapter 4:

Consciousness

Your level of consciousness creates your personal reality

We're all born with a different purpose and lessons that we were meant to grow from.

Knowing that our biggest struggles and pains are our key strengths can give us the highest insights once we have overcome them. Leaders are born through adversity and will gain the capability to create the life that they truly deserve.

Consciousness can be viewed as awareness of the energy level that we are living in.

Consciousness is critical for profound success in life; once we are aware of our level of energy, we can also be mindful of the level of energy that we bring into situations and when meeting the right partner.

A conscious relationship is when you can understand your partner and see what is needed to make the relationship flourish and grow.

We often get into unconscious relationships with people in which we only consider our own needs and what they can provide for us. However, this type of relationship isn't healthy because it neglects the other person's feelings or desires.

When I first understood consciousness, it fascinated me because I thought I was already aware of myself. I believed internally that I was aware of what was happening around me and my circumstance, and that circumstance was 'shit.' I was aware that I was depressed, sad, and stuck in a bad situation.

I had a belief that I only invite bad things into my life. When I thought that way, I carried a victim mentality, a perspective that everything was against me. Life became a fight, and I always seemed to lose.

Becoming aware and more conscious allowed me to understand that the bad things that happen to us are meant to happen for us to grow, learn and enable ourselves to create a better life.

The book Your Souls Plan discusses how we can arrange for things to happen to develop and become more robust, caring, and less naive.

When I started looking at the world from a perspective, in which I'd ask myself during bad situations, 'what can I learn from this? What can I take from this situation?', my life began to turn around as I became the creator of my experiences.

I applied this level of thinking to every aspect of my life.

I was dating someone and started to build more courage and confidence within me; as I dated her, things were beginning to go well, but the people I loved the most, my brother and mother were completely against our relationship.

They were abusive and very aggressive towards the person I was dating. I was clueless at the time as to why anyone would want to treat someone like this when they haven't done anything wrong. I started questioning myself as my victim mentality returned and made me think that it was all my fault.

I was down and confused about why this would happen to me. I felt like my family was trying to ruin my life. It was hard for me to stay focused at work, and it was difficult for me to be without the love of my life.

Until I decided to step up and refused to continue to live like this. I learned to grow and become more of who I am. I took accountability for my life, and I stepped into a powerful state of consciousness.

I invested in myself by getting a coach; I worked on being a better me and began to take lead of my emotions. I became the man I was meant to be because of the difficulties I faced in that situation.

Looking back, I can see that the situation was a gift to help me grow and be a leader. I was meant to learn to be strong, decisive, and loving the past events created my character.

These bad situations help you become a better version of yourself. If you're going through a hard time, a difficult situation, it's okay, and I want you to understand that this is meant to make you more extraordinary.

Most importantly, we must heed the lessons from such negative situations to ensure they don't repeat. Remember, these situations are only temporary, but the learning we can take from them can last all our lives and be passed down to our children.

Understanding this vital principle will lead you to a higher level of consciousness. So, next time you are placed within a negative situation, try to determine the lessons you can pick up.

Dimensional therapy is one of the biggest gifts I can share with any client. It helps them let go of any pains and struggles they've had in their lives for them to see their life from a different perspective.

Dimensional therapy combines hypnotic trance, NLP, and timeline therapy. Numerous clients have created the life they want by going through this therapy. It is a transformational therapy that I have made that allows you to create a new meaning to your life, connecting with your subconscious mind. You will be free from the past to create the life you want to live.

All subconscious patterns running within our lives are formed between 0-7 years old from past generations or past lives (based on people's beliefs). The subconscious mind is responsible for 95% of the running of our lives, and it runs our day-to-day behaviours. So, therefore, if we can change any of these negative patterns by understanding the subconscious mind even more deeply than ever before, we will be able to live the life we want and how we want to live it.

One of the roles of the subconscious mind is to store negative thoughts and hide them away from us, to protect us from the pains of the past.

It also stores other memories and habitual actions needed for day-to-day activities. Therefore, old patterns of a past relationship may appear, affecting how you behave in certain situations, even after entering a newer relationship.

E.g., imagine if your whole family carries a habit of eating junk foods late at night. You'll begin to believe that it is considered the norm. Slowly, you too may accept this behaviour and begin to follow it. If it becomes a habitual pattern, you will have passed down evidence to your mind that eating junk foods late at night is okay. Your mind will now develop a new belief that will encourage your habit.

To break this habit, you'd need to become more aware of its adverse effects. Gaining more awareness as to how these foods can hurt your health, such as by listening to the stories of others, will enable you to let go of this habit.

When we have an undealt problem, our subconscious mind will hide it; our view and judgment on situations will still be influenced by these hidden memories. In addition, these repressed memories are where our gut feeling is derived from, and our gut feeling is a warning from the subconscious mind. As such, if you've had a painful or hurtful experience, the memory itself will not disappear.

To bring more profound love and connection into our lives, we must learn from the past and grow from our negative experiences. Once we change the meaning of these events, we will be able to transmute the energy and become a better version of ourselves. This will allow us to let go of any subconscious blocks within our relationships.

Dimensional therapy can release traumas and pains and heal them by transmuting the energy to that of a higher vibration. In other words, it allows you to be free from the past, if you learn from these memories.

Changing the way, you perceive the original event of pain and suffering will allow you to learn the lessons and be able to transmute the energy to be free from pain and any blocks.

Imagine: God, the higher being, is trying to give you a sign of love, trying to tell you: 'you have to change your path, you have to change what you're doing.'

You're on the wrong path. If you don't listen to the sign, it may receive a stronger message to tell you to wake up; 'it's time to make a change.' However, if you still don't listen, then the light energy may go to the dark side and say,

Could you do a favour for me?
I need you to wake this person up.
We need them to evolve and change.
And now, by doing this, there'll be an event, a more profound event that happens in your life.

Now, a significant event will create a change in your life, and this change will be significant enough for you to make that evolution in your own life to change your pathway.

I want you to reflect on your life. Has there been a time when you went through a callous time, and since then, you have been able to create more with your life?

We can be everything we want to be, and sometimes, the universe, God, infinite intelligence put the challenges in life for us to grow and be more.

Jade went through a tough time two years ago. She was suffering and was in a bad place, her partner had cheated on her, and she lost who she was.

She fell into a depression without knowing. She would hide in her room, overeat, abuse alcohol to cover up some of her feelings. She was not living up to her full potential, and as a result, she wasn't taking care of her health.

She gained a lot of weight and stayed in bed all day and night.

Soon after, she was fired from work for not hitting targets and being too preoccupied at work. Then things got worse for her, and she started to stay away from friends and family, making up excuses not to meet them until one day, she decided that enough was enough, that she was going to make a change.

She went out for a run and fell and hurt her leg, and she had to go to the hospital. When she got to the hospital, she was scared, not knowing how bad it would be.

The hospital found blood clots in her leg; she had to do an operation on her leg and connect the nerves to the foot again; otherwise, her foot could have been amputated. She was worried that she might not walk again. She went through pain, hurt, and worry.

Thankfully, the doctors did a fantastic job, but she realized that all the things she was holding on to were holding her back from being the person she is.

She went back home and started to rebuild who she was. She told her family and friends that she loved them and appreciated everyone around her. It was like her whole life had changed. She became present and forgot about everything else.

She appreciated everyone and everything around her, she came from a full heart, and nothing else from the past mattered. She is now very healthy and has a great job and a great relationship with her family, and she went on a journey of learning about herself to become more.

This is an example of how the darkness could be the architect of your life to help in a situation where you can change and grow. If we learn the lessons, we won't need to repeat the experience.

Now, it is important to let go of all the anger, hurt, sadness, guilt, and pain that you may have in your life. Some of the key learnings that many clients get are not your pain or guilt; it was passed on to you.

Another key learning is that they are loved and protected; even if it is hard to see, it is possible to realize that someone did love you if it was a mother, a friend, or anyone.

They believed that they were good enough to truly live the life they deserved to become more of them.

Task:

Knowing that the past problems were lessons, I would like you to write down the positive learning you can get from the past. How did it make you stronger?
What was the greater purpose of these events?

_____

_____

_____

_____

Chapter 5

Your identity is who you are.

"Whether you think you can,
or you think you can't--
you're right."
Henry Ford

Your identity is the underlying factor that will lead you to achieve any results you want in life as we subconsciously align ourselves with our identity.

If you say that you are deficient in relationships, then this is an identity that you have created or if you say you find love easy, this is another identity.

When we create empowering identities for ourselves, our subconscious minds will match the essence, and we will be able to create love faster.

If your identity is such that you're bad in relationships, then naturally, our subconscious and conscious mind will find all the reasons why we are bad in relationships. Then when you get mistreated in relationships, you will accept it because you believe that this is who you are.

If somebody has an identity in which they tell themselves that they don't deserve love, they will also resist receiving love when love does come into them. They will reject the love others give them as they believe they do not deserve it.

The truth is, that is all BS; because you have had some bad relationships in the past, they should do not define your future relationships.

You have the power to transform and change your love destiny at any given moment, and it all starts with your identity.

Your identity becomes your vibrational home.

In this chapter, we will create an identity that reflects your most powerful self, which will set you on the correct path on your relationship journey.

Having a clear picture of your identity can help you step into your powerful self every day.

When do you need to use your powerful identity?

Before going on a date with a potential partner or interacting with someone:

 how would you show up if you held an identity in which you continually told yourself, 'I don't deserve love?' When you speak, perhaps you'd feel self-doubt or wouldn't accept the compliments given. The reason why we believe these things is because we don't believe in who we are.

What type of energy would you be emitting out there to the world?

'I'm not worthy of love, low energy, and pity.'

If you are the type to attract narcissistic people, you allow them to take the lead of your energy, which is why you attract them into your life.

If we have low energy, we start taking actions that reflect it. When you text each other, being too kind, not valuing your boundaries, and allowing them to walk all over you.

Sending photos that we do not want to, to try and get their attention. These are all linked to having a low identity of yourself. It's time for you to recognize your greatness and become the creator of your love life.

Another identity many people take on:

The independent 'I don't need love' identity.

It is a stronger identity to the 'I don't deserve love' identity because now you are in control of your relationship destiny (or so we believe). The issue with this identity is a wall over the heart, which protects you from getting hurt and stops you from genuinely loving another person.

Someone with this identity will tend to search for the one and find faults with others to protect themselves. They believe that others are too good to be true and will leave the relationship once they find any issues with the person they meet.

These beliefs are sometimes passed down to us, and sometimes we create these beliefs. These beliefs sabotage growth and our ability to find lasting love as we always blame the external rather than looking within.

Compared to having absolute confidence and empowering inner believes that know your worth and that you truly deserve love.

My expertise with NLP has allowed me to understand the keys to creating your identity. We will understand exactly what someone's identity is made up of and how we can create it to be better.

The Four factors that make up the identity.

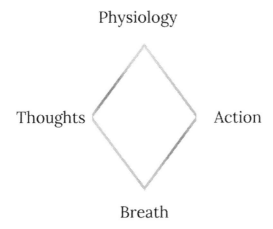

Physiology

Thoughts

Action

Breath

The first factor is our physiology, the way that we stand. Power Posing was first introduced by Amy Cuddy in 2010 when she suggested that standing in "high power" produces power by increasing testosterone and decreasing cortisol levels.

While recent studies have been unable to reproduce these findings to that extent, they suggest that power posing affects confidence and stress levels.

- In one study, High power posers were more likely to assume risk and gamble (86% vs. 60%), whereas low-power posers played it safe. The high-power posers also demonstrated increased testosterone and decreased cortisol levels and reported feeling more powerful (2.57 vs. 1.83 out of 5) after posing.
- In another study, before a mock interview, participants were instructed to perform a high-power pose or a low power pose. The high-power posers received significantly higher scores on hireability and performance. They maintained their composure, projected more confidence, and presented more captivating and enthusiastic speeches.

Just do it for a minute.

I would like you to stand up and take up a power pose!

How would your shoulders be?
How would your head be? Up or down?
How would your chest be? Down or up?

Take some deep breaths and observe and notice. Do you feel like you have more confidence, more energy, or less?

Now I would like you to take up a negative pose:
Poor position, perhaps your head is down
Your shoulders are down
You are not breathing as deep
Observe how your energy is in this new position.

It is essential to be aware of your posture to feel confident when you have a strong identity.

The second part, once our physiology and body are positive.

Breathe - The breath of life

In yoga and Indian background, prana is the life force that comes through us. In Sanskrit, it has been said before as "the breath of life." When you put your body into a good place with positive thoughts, like taking deep breaths while feeling relaxed or believing yourself to be at peace, this helps because it allows oxygenation throughout our entire system, which leads to many parts being energized due to their vibrant energy flowing freely again!

Right now, do it with me.

Take a deep breath in and hold it in your chest for four seconds.
And now breathe out for six seconds
And breath in again, holding it for 4 seconds
And out for 6 seconds

Feel and notice how relaxed you feel now.

When we are stressed, we usually breathe fast and heavy or do not breathe at all.

And when we're not getting this lifeforce, this breath into our body, we are creating even more anxiety and worry.

By managing our breath, it helps us to manage our emotional state.

Feeling - Thoughts = Creating the life we see

The thoughts we create about a particular area of life will affect how we act.

Our thoughts are the key to creating the life that we want, and I know sometimes we think the words that we say, which is also a big part, but before the words come the thoughts that we have, by going deeper into our thoughts that we choose to believe we start to create our outer world.

The thought we focus on creates our reality, and it starts within.

Visualizing allows us to expand the thoughts that we want to have in life and create more of the reality that we want to happen.

Most people manifest without knowing as we visualize the worst-case scenarios and play them out in our minds. It's time to envision what you want, not what you don't want. Therefore, we must realize what we're thinking and focusing on.

The more we focus on the life that we want and focus our thoughts on getting there, the more familiar we become with this reality, and it will match our vibration.

For example, if you have thoughts of:

I am lovable,
I am a magnet of love

And you are walking around believing these thoughts in your mind that if you saw somebody that looked at you, you would think they are attracted to you because you are the magnet of love.

These inner beliefs will impact how you are perceived in the world as you will be radiating, allowing others to acknowledge your presence.

You can see how having thoughts that no one would want me would lead to you thinking someone is judging me or laughing at me. Compared to the person that is attracted to you, based on your inner beliefs.

In a moment the world you see will be different, it will be full of opportunities, friends, and connection. Acknowledging that, yes, you are incredible, and you are unique can help you open to more opportunities.

The following side to the diamond of your identity is your language and actions.

Language and actions are essential to create your identity and show up in the world

The action that we take to start creating their lives is how our world will begin to change and become the way we want it to be, because if you feel great, look great, and own your identity, but we take no actions to move forward, then it is wasted, and many people do this. They read books and like the learning but do not implement it.

Taking risks and opportunities is key to growing the muscle of your identity.

Now, we want to use empowering words about ourselves and others, take action that will help you create more of this identity, and push yourself to be more.

If we do not take the right action or use the right words, we will not honour the identity and fall back under old patterns. If we act from the old identity, we will match that again.

More specifically if somebody is anxious.

How would this anxious person approach a situation, what language and actions would they take.

They may feel good and believe that others like them and radiate beautiful energy. They also have good physiology. Their chest is out, and their head is up. They are breathing correctly, breathing in a strong, beautiful, calm way.

But the actions and language are still of anxious state:

Perhaps their language of words will be low and quiet.
They will miss opportunities and not act.
They might not be able to communicate.

Rather than, communicating from a certain place within, knowing you have value to add to others. It is important for them to hear your perspective on the world.

Someone who knows their worth and knows they are enough has these beliefs inside their head that they are worthy of love.

https://www.researchgate.net/publication/320925193_Posture_and_Social_Problem_Solving_Self-Esteem_and_Optimism - Amy Cudd

What actions and language would they use?

Action would be to be out there to communicate with this person to approach them, talk to them, and then when they speak to them, what kind of language would they use, or are they direct, confident, funny, cheeky, witty?

Language is an essential part of our identity. Using the NLP communication model shows that words are only 7% of communication with somebody, 38% Is the tone of voice. And 55% is their physiology and the energy you put into this.

Task: Write down what actions would you take if you were confident?

How would you communicate?
How would you stand?
What thoughts would you have about yourself and others?

What tone would you have? Are you communicating with a negative tone, an angry tone? or a sad tone?
How would it sound in a loving voice? Or a joyful voice?

The energy that we put into communication dictates the emotion carried across. I ultimately know what energy it's coming from. Has there ever been a time in your life where that's happened as well?

The language in how we speak and communicate is important. The frequency and vibration of our communication, many discoveries show that their frequency and the tone that we speak out is a vibration that we send to the world.

Sending this vibration to the world is how it returns to us. If we're speaking from a low vibration and asking for a relationship, we send out a low tone, and this sound wave still gets sent to the world. However, it returns even slower.

When we send it with higher energy and higher vibration, the sound wave will be sent out and returned a lot faster.

Vibrational alignment means the energy you are sending out is vibrating at the same frequency as the energy you desire to experience. The most effective way to know what vibration you are currently in is through your feelings and emotions.

Rules and Values of Life

The rules and values of life are one of the most powerful exercises you can complete to transform your life. When re-writing the rules around your life, you can truly change the game of life to ensure you are winning.

Your rules and values create your life map, and they influence how you live your life and your ability to be successful. We will now develop new rules and values that serve us to be more alive and awaken the lover.

When I first discovered this in our NLP, I found that the rules that I had in my life were making me unhappy. They were sabotaging who I was, pulling me down, and not allowing me to be the best version of myself.

They were making me give my power away to others; when I learned how to change this, I started taking control. I started to become the power; that is why I created a passionate, loving relationship because it all started with me.

We all have core values and core emotions. For example, a core value could be joy, love, or success.

The core values we want to have in life help us get to where we want.

If someone's core value is freedom, it will have a completely different outcome to someone who has a life that values love number one.

If you value freedom, then you will do anything to have it. This sometimes means that we will want to be free above anything else, which means when we are in a relationship and our freedom is limited, we will move away from the relationship without knowing as our core value in life is not being met.

If you value love, you will do anything to feel that emotion, and this means that you'll do more to feel love in your life, around family, friends and we will make sacrifices to be in a relationship.

There are many core values that we could think about, but here are some of the common ones;

1 . Freedom
2 . Love
3 . Happiness
4 . Luck
5 . Self-Worth
6 . Security
7 . Entrepreneur
8 . Courage
9 . Freedom
10. Success

And these are just examples. There are many more to choose from.

Once again, notice how each word feels different when you're reading them out loud? Notice which one resonates with you.

Understanding these core values helps us understand what we want from a relationship, what will be important in your life, and relationships.

If you have a core value of respect, your life will be different from someone that wants happiness.

If someone's core value is respect, they may have a hard exterior and demand respect from another, even controlling situations to feel respected.

If feeling loved in a relationship is vital for you, we must understand what needs to happen to feel loved?

For example, suppose somebody whose core value was to be appreciated, and another is love.

In that case, one will value time together over being thanked for how they are in the relationship. This could cause difficulties in the relationship as they won't be aligned.

The next thing we look at is:

What needs to happen for you to achieve this value?

What needs to happen to feel the value is the rules for the value; the more rules you have, the harder it will be for you to feel the value.

So, if a person wants to be appreciated as a top value, we will need to understand their rules; what needs to happen to feel appreciated?

If it was for person one to feel appreciated, they need to be taken out, and they will need to be told how amazing they are, and they will need to receive gifts and calls to feel appreciated.

Looking at the value of appreciation, we can understand that it will be difficult for somebody to appreciate this person without taking them out without buying them things. Then we also need to consider, how often does this need to happen?

Perhaps it could be all the time that they need to be taken out to be given kind words to be looked after. You can understand how this could be frustrating for your partner who wants to love.

Their rule for love is to spend time together, kiss, be intimate, and be told I love you. You can see how both people can experience love differently and not feel loved as they want the relationship to have a different feeling.

If the rules were different, if they had a rule that worked internally rather than externally, they could have a different level of love, happiness, and fulfilment within the relationship.

If we trade our wants for appreciation, the relationship will have harmony.

Shakespeare said;

I always feel happy, you know why? Because I don't expect anything from anyone, expectations always hurt. Life is short. So love your life. Be happy. And keep smiling.

Just live for yourself and always remember:

Before you speak, Listen,
Before you write, Think,
Before you spend, Earn,
Before you pray, Forgive,
Before you hurt, Feel,
Before you hate, Love,
Before you quit, Try,
Before you die, Live.

Imagine feeling fulfilled within the relationship based on your own rules. How amazing would life be and feel for the level of happiness to be based on you?

By changing our rules around life, we can create more fulfilment and enjoy life whilst creating an exciting life and relationship.

We cannot give from an empty cup, but we can give in abundance from a full cup.

Imagine how life would be when you feel complete?
Full of love, appreciation, connection.

What would you be able to do if you felt whole and complete?

The key to creating a long-lasting relationship is being free from any co-dependencies and being able to take the lead of your emotional state, making your happiness within and creating a conscious relationship together.

Task: I'd like you to write down below.

What are your core values? What is most important for you
to feel when in a relationship?
Loved
Safe
Connected

_____
_____
_____
_____
_____
_____
_____
_____
_____

Then what needs to happen for you to feel this way
I would like you to make it easy by using
anytime and or when writing this down.

E.g.:
I feel loved anytime I think of someone that I care about
or
I feel love whenever I see love in the world
Or
I feel loved whenever I am grateful for the people in my life
See how we are making it very easy to feel loved, and
therefore, we can receive love easily and give love easily as
the cup is full.

I would like you to think about how much of a change this
will have in your life.

Imagine five years from now being in a relationship with an amazing partner, and instead of demanding love or appreciation from them, you feel it within.

In the past, you may have had rules that were to be treated and brought gifts to feel loved but instead of having these things happen to feel loved, you feel loved, and then you can appreciate even more the bonuses of the relationship.

Quantum physics has found that similar atoms are automatically attracted to each other. This is the same with our body cells. When we radiate more love, it is easier to attract, and just like when we radiate anger, we can fight EVERYWHERE!

The trick here is to make life easy to feel the things we want to feel and meet our core values. By meeting your core values, you will feel happier, loved, important, appreciated within and wouldn't need to demand it externally.

This would allow you to set bigger goals in life and create more positive excitement within the relationship.

Once your core values are met, you will feel fulfilled within the relationship and will be able to have a greater relationship.

Most of the time, when we are switching off from a relationship, we are not being fulfilled within the relationship.

Let's break down what will be needed in your life to create the identity to create the love destiny that is wanted.

When we look at singles, these are the most common archetypes that come up:

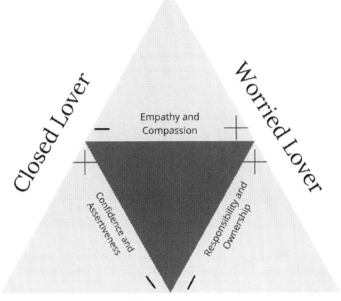

Closed Lover

Worried Lover

Empathy and
Compassion

Confidence and
Assertiveness

Responsibility and
Ownership

Suffering Lover

The closed lover:

The closed lover is strong, rebuilt from pains and struggles but doesn't want to experience hardship again.

Closed Lover To Passionate Lover

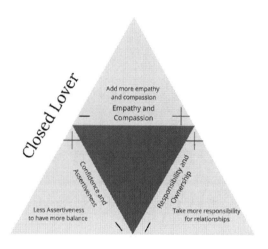

This person struggles to have empathy and compassion for others because of the pain experienced in the past. Want to experience love but have a deep-down fear to not let love in. Struggles with compassion and empathy and struggles to connect with their feelings pass on the ownership and responsibility of relationships to others.

They're missing compassion and empathy for others, and they need to take ownership and responsibility for the relationships in their lives. The closed lover believes that it is the other person's fault, they are unable to find the right partner, and the relationship didn't work because of them.

The key to tremendous relationship success is to take more responsibility and ownership for their relationships and have more empathy and compassion for themselves and others.

When this is done, we start seeing them blossom into a passionate lover, a leader within the relationship, and somebody that can connect and bring love in at the deepest level.

The worried lover:

Worried Lover To Impactful Lover

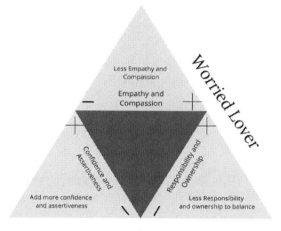

The worried lover takes too much ownership and responsibility, for relationships and understands their partners needs above their own. A high level of empathy and compassion is limiting them and putting their partners on a pedal stool.

The worried lover needs to reduce the amount of ownership and responsibility in relationships, causing them to worry. It is essential to find a good balance point of how much they are taking on and how much is their partners responsibility. Also, Reduce the amount of empathy and compassion they give to others and start increasing the compassion they give to themselves.

The key to relationship success is to add on assertiveness and inner confidence. This can be done by believing in themselves and setting boundaries, communicating the boundaries to partners to help them become impactful lovers. Now, they become a strong, caring lover that is appreciated.

Then we have the suffering lover.

Suffering Lover To Love Creator

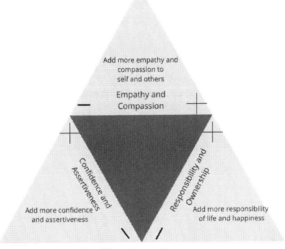

Suffering Lover

The suffering lover has been stung in the past, and this pain is still hurting them not to love; living in pain is hindering their life. The suffering lover is lacking ownership of relationships, empathy for themselves or others and haven't developed the assertiveness to stand up for themselves.

The suffering lover needs to let go of the pains of the past and take more responsibility and ownership for life and relationships, acknowledging that there was a greater learning from the past relationships. Have more confidence within and assertiveness to be clear with what they tolerate within a relationship.

Adding, more compassion and empathy for others and themselves will allow them to become the creator of love they seek in the world and give more love to others rather than making love.

When they evolve, you will go from Victim to Victor.

When we put in the strength, compassion, empathy, ownership, and assertiveness within ourselves and others, we start creating the love you truly deserve at the highest levels.

These patterns that form who we are could be a learned behaviour, passed down, or pain from a young person. It is usually a subconscious blueprint that is installed in our programming, once you become aware of which identity you were, you could change the blueprint to create the love you want.

I would like you to highlight which lover you match the most?

_____
_____
_____

What is needed for your love life to be better and for you to create the love you want?

_____
_____
_____
_____

Task: I would like you to write down who were you in the past?
Suffering lover, Closed lover, or worried lover?

What do you need to add more of to help your love journey?
Do you need more ownership and responsibility?
Do you need more empathy and compassion to take you to the next level?
Or have you been a worried lover where you need to be more assertive, need to take less responsibility, and have less empathy for you to get to the next level?

_____
_____
_____
_____

This is how Aron implemented this learning:

Aron was a closed lover in the past and had negative beliefs. He took more responsibility for his relationships and had empathy and compassion for future relationships. He decided to implement it by understanding his friends and family more and creating a deeper relationship.

His new beliefs are.

Many amazing partners are out there; they will work through problems together to create a passionate relationship.

This is how Sharon implemented this learning.

Sharon was a worried lover. She took too much responsibility for relationships she had, cared about people too much, and took ownership of their mistakes.

She learned to strive to be an impactful lover, giving love but not taking on too much responsibility. She cared but found a good balance. The key breakthrough was when she knew she had to have more confidence and assertiveness to help her create more love.

Believing she is worthy of love, she is the creator of her love, and she is good enough for the right partner.

This is how Jade implemented this learning:

Jade realized that she had a suffering lover approach to relationships due to past relationships, and she has a new understanding to be able to be a creator of her love. She will need to have more confidence, assertiveness, empathy, compassion, and ownership of her life.

Chapter: 6:

The creator of love

Love someone for no reason

Most people put conditions on love,
limiting the amount of love
and holding themselves back.
This isn't LOVE. It's FEAR

The Dalai Lama said, whenever you feel crushed, under pressure, or in darkness, you're in a powerful place for transformation and transmutation.

Imagine a world where all the people are flourishing. This would be an amazing place to live in, right? Now imagine if we could make this happen by changing our vibrational frequency!

We all have the power to change our vibration in the world; it is not the environment that creates our vibration. It is based on our focus and intention. The vibrational energy that we have makes our life, and if it is low, we will attract negative experiences and use forceful energy.

When someone is living in the desire to want many things, it is an excellent intention to want more; however, it limits them as they feel they do not have enough in present state, which creates forceful energy of lack.

The journey that we're going to go on in this chapter has truly been able to change my own life as well as my clients' lives, to be able to become the creators of their life.

Energy is everything; as the great Albert Einstein said, it is the most crucial area of life to master. Once you can become conscious of the energy you are vibrating at in the world, you will create the life you want.

There are different energy stages, and when we are stuck energy in an area of life, it will affect the results. Changing the energy in each area will change the results you get.

We all have the power to create our reality, but do you know how? The answer is within us. The outside world shapes us and helps us build a character; however, it changes our reality of the world. We discover that we have limitless potential for growth and happiness when we look within!

Your Personality Creates Your Personal Reality

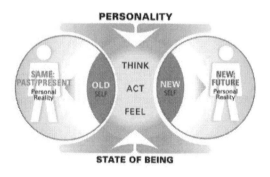

Reference: Dr Joe Dispenza – you are the placebo

The physical world is a distortion of your thoughts. When you are in traumatic or painful situations, these experiences affect how things look and feel for us outside them because we distort what's really happening with our minds after the fact based on past traumas.

It is why many people live in fear due to a previous significant event that has impacted them, and now they are seeing the world through this lens. Once you can change the lens, it allows you to see the same situation with a fresh pair of eyes; it could be information-based down to you or an accident you experienced yourself.

When we transmute that energy of the past and lift it, we can see clearly again. We can put the right energy to carry a frequency and intention to get us to the goal that we want.

'If every atom is 99.9999999999999 percent energy or information, that means that our known universe and everything in it—independently of how solid that matter may appear to us—is essentially just energy and information.' Dr Joe Dispenza.

Understanding this will allow us to step into a new level of energy to create from any level of life.

Quantum physics has proven that our thoughts manifest into the world. Some studies show that we can attract more of what we want when intention and emotion are aligned.

When we look at this, we're going to break down the main areas: the thoughts, habits, beliefs, and feelings, empowering us to create a stronger identity.

Breaking down these areas will make you an expert in your state when creating love.

Dr. David Hawkin speaks about consciousness and energy, that flows through us which creates our conscious life that we life.

God view	Life view	Level	Log	Emotion	Process
		Map of Consciousness by David R. Hawkins			
Self	Is	Enlightenment	700-1000	Ineffable	Pure Consciousness
All-Being	Perfect	Peace	600	Bliss	Illumination
One	Complete	Joy	540	Serenity	Transfiguration
Loving	Benign	Love	500	Reverence	Revelation
Wise	Meaningful	Reason	400	Understanding	Abstraction
Merciful	Harmonious	Acceptance	350	Forgiveness	Transcendence
Inspiring	Hopeful	Willingness	310	Optimism	Intention
Enabling	Satisfactory	Neutrality	250	Trust	Release
Permitting	Feasible	Courage	200	Affirmation	Empowerment
Indifferent	Demanding	Pride	175	Scorn	Inflation
Vengeful	Antagonistic	Anger	150	Hate	Aggression
Denying	Disappointing	Desire	125	Craving	Enslavement
Punitive	Frightening	Fear	100	Anxiety	Withdrawal
Disdainful	Tragic	Grief	75	Regret	Despondency
Condemning	Hopeless	Apathy	50	Despair	Abdication
Vindictive	Evil	Guilt	30	Blame	Destruction
Despising	Miserable	Shame	20	Humiliation	Elimination

Expansive states (giving energy)
Contracting (taking energy)

David Hawkins was able to muscle test participants to measure their muscle energy, testing the vibrational strength within the body when in different states.

Muscle testing is where you hold your arm up and can test the subconscious and the greater thinking of yourself to understand what energy is being transmuted into that frequency that is out there.

He measured the destructive and creative energies to show which level gives more energy to our body or less.

Creative energy is based on a higher energy source that goes through our bodies. It was measured using kinesiology and muscle testing techniques to determine the results. The lower emotions showed a weak effect and a force to sustain strength when tested.

The destructive energies go all the way from shame to pride. These are classified as forceful due to the lower vibration and energy created using these emotions. These emotions limit us from being our true selves as it we do not use the creative energy within us. They negatively impact the world and the areas you focus your time on.

The emotions of courage and above are the creative energy. They create a higher vibration in the world and your life. Being courageous means that we are willing to take responsibility and make decisions, even if the outcome is unknown. Courage also refers to our ability to open up in relationships and be vulnerable with others around us.

The suffering lover's identity is at the vibrational level of apathy and shame. This emotional home believes that it is always their fault. No one would love them. The apathy is a feeling that I'm not good enough to receive anything. It's a hopeless feeling inside. We can see that it is at a low vibrational level.

Dr Hawkins – Power vs Force

Imagine this level of energy being put into relationships or dating. There will be poor results as the energy going in is limited. This low vibrational energy doesn't allow us to attract what we want or draw in relationships in life.

It is dangerous to date when you have low energy; it opens you up to narcissists and manipulators because they will see an easy opportunity to take the lead of your energy. It is crucial to have the courage to express and be open when you are uncomfortable within relationships, as this will remove any toxic individuals from your life.

Understanding this is the key to evolving to the next level.

The worried lover constantly has an emotional home of fear, anxiety, and grief. Every day they question, "What if things go wrong?" or even worse: "How do I recover from another broken heart?".

While focusing on the worst-case scenario creates low energy and poor actions within the relationship, which creates a connection of control, insecurities, and expectations of how the other person should act.

This falls under the levels of fear, grief, and desire. They want a relationship to work. However, fear is holding them back from creating the love they want.

At this level, the beliefs are 'what if they hurt me, what if I'm not good enough for them.' Perhaps they have taken on too much responsibility for relationships not working out in the past, which has led to further self-blame and lack of self-belief.

In this state, the person will take on too much responsibility. The physiology will be very low, pulled down, shoulders down, and weak in the language that comes out. Friendships will be there at this level, but it would be hard to maintain deep friendships as some may move away from them.

Actions in relationships will be messaging too much, overthinking about the partner, and controlling the relationship based on fear.

This is destructive energy taken from relationships rather than given to them. The vibrational level is between 75 - 125. Although it is greater than the energy of the same and the suffering lover, it is still destructive.

Newton's law was based on evidence of the past. While we focus on this past energy, it will create more future. Quantum physics focuses on creating the future now, letting go of the past, and creating your own identity to have what you want.

It will be important for anyone in the worried lover state to let go of past fears and live in the energy they want for the future.

The closed lover also has insecurities, fears, and doubts about relationships; however, instead of being worried about them, they form a defence to deflect it onto others. They begin to project their fears.

We now look at the energy of desire, anger, and pride. It forms the closed lover. They tend to blame the external circumstances when life isn't working for us and how we want it to be.

When we start blaming the outside, we are not taking responsibility for what is happening in life. Believing 'it is the other person's fault' and ' I'm too good for them' is hiding away from the growth within the experience. Being angry and blaming others leads to more pain and destruction within the world we create.

The closed lover will not deal with the deeper issues within relationships and will move away before it gets too tough, projecting their problems to others. It will push many people away, cause many fights, and stop growth for the future. It is more common for a closed lover to have the traits of a narcissist due to their behaviour when dealing with issues.

When anyone encounters fear, it forces them to act differently. It is essential to be aware of who you become when fear comes into the relationship. If you are projecting anger and blaming others, the way to solve these issues is to take responsibility for the problem.

Fear is an illusion; it is a construct and focus of the worst-case scenario in situations, faith is another construct of the mind focusing on the positive outcomes which can occur.

Choosing fear is easier as most of us operate from our survival brain, fear can benefit us by preparing us to be greater, but when you give too much energy to it, it will get the better of us. To let go of fear, we need to step back into that courage to overcome any of our fears.

When we are afraid in our lives, it limits us to be less than who we truly are. We become controlling, needy, ungrateful, and sabotage the relationship. Fear is when you start to expect your potential partner to be a certain way, which is the need for control.

Fear is when you start to dictate how your partner should be, or you start to run away from the world. Fear is the projection onto others and limiting yourself from opportunities.

Use courage and faith to break free from fear.

When we transition into courage, this is where we get into our creative energy, our creative flow. This energy will allow us to take steps to the relationship and love that you genuinely want. Courage allows us to be vulnerable, open to opportunities, and open to love.

Courage is the belief that I'm going to make this happen, and if it doesn't work out, it's okay; I tried.

Having this level of belief and confidence allows us to overcome any fear we have. It will enable us to step into a higher being, a higher person within ourselves.

This takes us to a place of readiness for a relationship. Readiness is when you are open and confident to be vulnerable to hurt, love, and connect rather than fearing them not liking you or feeling rejected.

Readiness is when you express yourself and put yourself outside of your comfort zone, knowing that you would grow and become more extraordinary if you were hurt. Being ready allows us to step into our higher creative energy, which takes the lead in life.

ALL PAIN IS CAUSED BY THE ILLUSION OF SUFFERING

Separation is caused by focusing on I, each destructive emotion from shame to pride, having a self-focus. These emotions create a wall that only focuses on ourselves and doesn't open space for others and grow.

Each of the beliefs is focused on I.

I am bad in relationships
I am scared,
I am worried.
I am too good.
No one wants me.

These are all reflections of the I, causing separation from others. When we let go of I and acknowledge others, we have a greater energy level.

When we step into courage, it's the courage to put ourselves out there for more and create love with others.

The more we move up the levels, the more we can see a greater energy level than we have.

I have the courage to connect with more. I have the courage to be in this relationship. I have the courage to date. If it doesn't work out, it's okay. That is courage. But it's about more than one. It's about opening up to bringing in more people.

When we look at neutrality and willingness, this energy is about knowing that everything is happening at the right time, knowing that everything will work out, and trusting the process.

Trusting who you are, trusting how life will work out for you in relationships, and accepting who you are to these kinds of levels of beauty.

We must accept ourselves to believe in ourselves enough that if one person wasn't attracted to you, you trust and accept that the right person is coming into your life.

The transition to mastery, becoming the master of your life and using a power to create the world you live in.

Once you accept yourself, you let go of the past and enjoy the journey you are creating—accepting all your greatness to share with the world and know yourself.

This is a vibrational level of 350. It allows you to be a creator of the life you want to have by setting goals and taking action to achieve them.

The next level of evolution is the vibration of love, and joy vibrates from 500 to 540. This state can be the magnet for what is wanted in life. This vibrational state feels unconditional love for others and receives deep love.

The belief that you are: You are the source of love. It is the energy of compassion and kindness that can enjoy life and the greatness of the experiences that happen. Action of expressing love and sharing compassion with others.

The success formula

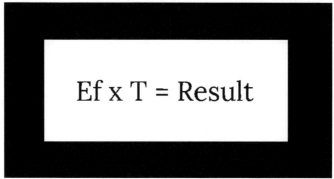

Energy (focus area) x Time = Result

The success formula is based on the energy you put into the focused area x time, which I mean present time (not multitasking) will equal the result you want in that area of life.

The present time is when you focus and give your energy to one thing at a time.

When you put loving energy into anything you do, you create more significant results; let's think about when you love the job you do; you will produce excellent results. Loving energy can transform your results.

When people feel happy, fulfilled, or content, all aspects of their lives start to improve because they're putting out good vibes everywhere, including at home. Others in proximity will follow suit in response due to the powerful hormonal reaction caused by oxytocin - aka "the love hormone."

You allow yourself and open yourself up to connecting to having a high level of energy to becoming more than any of your circumstances AND becoming who you are.

When you add this loving energy into the world of sharing love with others and joy, the universe will send more love in your direction.

Have you ever had a job that you loved?

You were excited to work there, enjoyed the job, and loved the people, you would get great results, but when a manager put fear into the role, you started to hate it and not enjoy it as much and start to get adverse effects at the place.

When we love dating and relationships, we get incredible results; the results will be more significant when you have a higher energy vibration in any given area. You will be able to attract more of what you want.

Task: what level of energy do you want to be?

_____

_____

What level of energy are you currently?

_____

_____

What do you need to let go of to move on to higher energy?

_____

_____

What level of energy do you want to share in your relationship?

_____

If you put a higher level of energy into life, friends, health, relationships, business, what level of results would you get?

_____

_____

_____

_____

_____

Let's test this, I would like you to think of an area of life that is going well, and I want you to think, what level of energy do you put into that area?

Most of the time, you will find it is of a higher energy source, either loving what you do or being brave enough to put yourself out there.

If you are going on a dating site, and you put the energy of fear into it, perhaps you get poor results because of the level of energy you are putting into it.

You may not open as much or be vulnerable with the person as you feel hurt from the past.

Whereas if you put the energy of courage into dating and be yourself, be funny, be outgoing, and maybe a little cheeky. Then imagine the energy that you'll get from putting this energy in.

Believing the right person is coming your way.

Imagine you remember that it is one step closer to finding the right partner every time you meet someone you didn't connect with. How would this outlook impact your dating life?

Imagine if the most significant partner stepped into your life, your King or Queen; what level of energy would you need to be at to connect with them?

One of the greatest lessons that I learned is 'when you take, the universe takes from you.'

If you're taking energy from others, taking, pulling their energy, and you're not giving back, you will be stealing from them, and then the universe will take from you.

When you give to the universe your energy and gifts to the world, the universe will give.

My client Sharon identified with this; she understood in the past, she took energy by living in the emotion of fear, sometimes the victim, and sometimes being nervous. It pulled the people's energy close to her, and the behaviour wasn't deliberate. It had developed throughout her life. Sharon often got love when she was in this state, which encouraged her brain to continue.

Sharon has a massive breakthrough; she commented on being a giver of energy by adding value to situations, being open, and loving others while respecting herself.

She messaged her friends and told them how much I love you. It became a daily habit of expressing love and kindness to others.
Another client used this method and understood the concept of giving rather than taking. She was insecure,

ashamed of her weight, and worked to create the body she wanted. She worked on herself for many years, and even though she improved and had the body that she wanted, she still felt insecure.

She always focused on herself; she would think, 'what do others think of me' which made her judge herself and criticize herself. Every time she would dress up to impress people but feel insecure.

She learned to give energy and focus on them rather than herself; she went into the office, saw somebody she knew, and complimented him on his shirt, making it about them. When she showed love, she started giving compliments to other people she met. All these potential dates surrounded her.

There are no limitations to your energy, and the more energy you share and give, the more you will receive.

A taker will believe that if I give, then there'll be less of me, and I will need to take more. However, when we believe in the abundance formula, we know we will receive more by giving.

I'm going to challenge you to give love to 3 people you know and send a message of love to appreciate them for anything they are. It could be a family member, a business partner, a colleague, or somebody you're speaking to get to know wherever that is; whoever that is, send them a moment of love.

You'll be surprised to see the amount of love that you've received back from the universe.

Love is the key to manifesting the life you want!

Chapter: 7

Six keys to unlocking a lasting relationship.

*"Whenever we manage to love without
expectations, calculations, negotiations,
we are indeed in heaven."*
~ Rumi

Creating a passionate, loving relationship is mastery and
these keys help you to unlock the relationship at deeper
levels.

Specific keys make people work, that drive them in life, and
if we use the right keys, we will know how to create a deep
relationship.

Imagine trying to start a Ferrari with the wrong keys,
nothing will happen, and you wouldn't get the best out of
the car. As humans, we are also the same.

We have a set of keys that can make us work. Once we understand the formula that drives your future partner and us, you will create a powerful relationship.

I'm excited about what I am going to share with you. These keys have helped my clients to find the right partner and be able to maintain a strong relationship.

I'm going to tell you why me and my wife use this every month to audit our relationship. We get to understand who we are and what is missing from our relationship?

It helps us understand what we need to do more to keep the love and the excitement alive?

These are the fundamentals of all happy relationships based on human physiology. Once you master this chapter, you will create amazing relationships with anyone you meet.

You will understand what keys are essential to drive you and any relationship in your life. It will help you understand why relationships work and don't. When you unlock the relationship, love, passion, and excitement.

By mastering these keys, it help you to be an example of a relationship.

You're doing it for your children and your grandchildren. You're doing it for the people around you, inspiring them to live a better life of relationships.

I believe the days of being in a bad relationship and staying in one have gone! We now have more options and are not deciding to stay in poor relationships. This means that now we must all level up how we are in relationships to get to the next level of love.

We now have the capabilities and consciousness to create a meaningful relationship. I hope that this will allow you to create deeper conversations with your future partner and understand each other's needs with more clarity.

The six keys can unlock your relationship for you to gain control over the relationship you have for you to be the leader, to know when the relationship isn't working out and when it is.

I first came across these keys when my wife and I again had a relationship struggle. We were arguing and struggling to connect. We had to understand what was working at the start of the relationship and what we're not doing now.

I soon realized that I wasn't meeting her needs, and she wanted to drive the relationship in a different way, which made us argue all the time and struggle to spend a long time together.

6 KEYS TO A HAPPY RELATIONSHIP

Security

Special
'Number 1'

Surge
Progress within the
relationship

Spontenous

Sto'rgi
Greek for Love

Serve
To serve your
partners needs

The first key is the Key of Security:

This key of security enables your partner to feel secure within the relationship to know that you're there for them.

The second key is the key of spontaneity:

This key is fundamental to unlock the adventure and passion within the relationship. This key allows people to be more and allows each other to enjoy the passion and excitement of the relationship.

The third key of Specialness:

This key allows us to make our partner special and notice all our specialties within the relationship. Most people will do almost anything to feel special within the relationship.

The fourth key is the key of Storg'i:

Storg'i is the Greek word for love and feel connected with another. This key allows two people to connect on a deeper level and feel each other out to create magic at a soulful level. The key to love and connection is when two people come together, and they connect as they want.

The fifth key is to Surge

To surge within the relationship is the key to growth. To surge allows both partners to plan their future, grow in life, and grow their minds to become more.

This is a power key that enables relationships to appreciate the growth of one another and be able to grow through hard times. They form an infinite attachment, which means that we can surge, learn, and develop together.

The Sixth Key to Serve:

This key is to serve your partner's needs. This is when you put their needs first and have no expectations of what you will get in return. This key is one of the highest levels within a relationship.

Once we put our partner's needs first and understand what they need to feel fulfilled, even if it costs us time or energy, we still put their needs first. When we do this within a relationship, we create a beautiful, passionate, loving relationship. We can unlock the magic within the relationship.

When we use all six keys within a relationship, this relationship will never end. This relationship will be of the highest level of passion and love.

We're going into detail with each key to understanding the negatives and positives thoroughly.

Human psychology shows that we predominantly use two keys in relationships and life, which decide your blueprint of the world and relationships. If two people match their keys, it is a strong foundation for a long-lasting relationship.

Now, based on what you just read, I would like you to think of a good relationship in your life, perhaps your best friend or close relative and think. How many of these keys are being met with your relationship?

Do you use the key of safety and security, knowing that they're there for you?

Do you use the key of spontaneity, which shows that you will do adventurous things together?

Do you use a key of being special, that you know the two of you share a close bond?

The key of Storgi of love and connection that you both be connected?

The key of Surge is growing together, planning new things, and encouraging new growth.

The key to serving is when they need you; are you there for them?

How many of the keys were met?

It takes three keys being met to create an addiction to the relationship.

I know that all six keys are within my relationship with my best friend.

There's a key of security that I know is there for me if I need it. If I need to message him and need some support financially or anything, I know that he'll be there.

The key to spontaneity is there, where we book random trips away and randomly meet up and arrange these things.

The key of specialists is that we have a special bond and connection where we've been friends for over 16 years.

The key to Storgi is the connection. I love my best friend, like a brother, who is close to me.

The fifth key to surge. We always talk about developing, getting more promotions or growth within life, even within the family, together. They both got excited to grow together and understand each other's life.

The sixth key to keep serving is knowing he is always there for me, and he knows that I'm always there for him, to serve and give him my support whenever needed.

Now, I would like you to think of a negative relationship, perhaps a past partner or someone you don't like. How many of the keys were met when things started to go downhill?

If I think of a bad relationship, I remember I had a friend before who was part of my life in the past. We used to get on like a house on fire. But towards the end, there was some conflict, and we moved away from each other.

We grew apart, and I can see that our keys did not match. When I think about it, he would typically not be around much if I needed him towards the end of our relationship. I didn't feel secure or safe that he was a friend. The key to spontaneity, sometimes we wouldn't meet, so it was not positive.

There was no special connection. The only time special was if we had an argument or fight (we will further discuss this in the chapter). There was a connection from the past, but it was slim at the time.

As you can imagine, the key to surge wasn't available as we weren't sharing and connecting and opening about each other's lives or knowing about each other.

Finally, serving and putting each other's needs first in this relationship didn't happen as we lost focus of each other.

The good thing is, once we understand these keys, we can understand how to use them in any relationship that we want.

How can we create more passion, excitement, and joy in a relationship we have?

I want you to think about which two are the most important keys in your life for a relationship to work.

_____

_____

_____

_____

I'm going to break down each key and see how people can use them positively or negatively.

Key number one is security.

Positive:

To be secure within a relationship has many good positives. We can always be there for our partners, have consistent messaging, and show them that we are there for them.

Another way to show the security you are creating within the relationship is knowing that your partner is there for you. Marrying your partner is a form of meeting this key.

Negative:

Too much security in the relationship could get boring. There would be no room for fun or adventure. When you want to be certain about everything, it can control and limit the relationship.

You could form a habitual pattern, and when you stick to a routine, it could make the relationship die down.

A negative way to take security from a relationship is to control your partner. It happens when we think we are losing the security of the relationship, so we begin to control situations to gain security. However, it damages the relationship.

The way I look at this key is that if you are giving security, it is positive; if you are trying to get security from the relationship, it is negative.

The key to spontaneity:

It helps us create spontaneous adventure within the relationship, creating passion and fun. Again, this can have its positives and its negatives.

Positive:

When used correctly, this could be one of the best relationship keys, like sending sweet, fun messages to your partner, which is very beautiful.

This could be a random text or a random gift or act of goodness that helps them feel better or lifts their mood.

You can send a late-night message saying, 'I'm thinking of you. or you can book a trip away from each other, which is a fantastic way to unlock the key of being spontaneous.

Negative:

A negative way to meet that need to be spontaneous is to argue. Creating an argument is the most typical way people meet their spontaneous needs. When they argue, they create a spontaneous roller coaster in the relationship, followed by make-up time.

Another negative way to be spontaneous is not talking to somebody ignoring their messages. This way, we're trying to create a gap that says, I'm not going to talk to you, I'm going to create this gap and be spontaneous, and I'll randomly message you in the future.

This is a negative way because people don't know if it's a game or if it's true if it's real or not. However, it still triggers a response in the person you are getting to know and creates a feeling.

Another example is when couples have short-term breakups and threaten the relationship. As a result, this will impact the security within the relationship, leading to one partner becoming closed and even wanting to leave the relationship.

It is why it is essential to balance the two keys.

The third key of Specialness

When we go into this door of being special and making your partner feel special, it could be a fantastic gift to the relationship by empowering your partner. However, this could be a dangerous key when misused.

Positive:

Making your partner feel special is one of the most honourable ways to treat your partner. If you can help your partner, feel a million dollars, that she is the most beautiful woman in the world, or he is the funniest guy in the world. Then this will enrich and empower the relationship to grow close.

One of the main reasons relationships do not work after somebody has cheated is that they do not feel secure or special within the relationship. Not knowing if someone else is more special than you.

Negative:

The negative way you use this key is forcing them to see you are special by putting others down and believing that you are better than them. This often happens within relationships as one person would put the other down as they feel uncomfortable with their success.

Another way we get this attention is by pretending that someone else is attracted to us or creating opportunities for someone else to want us to have your partner fight for you.

This is an issue as it will work one or two times; however, the arguments will get worse and become more tempered as time goes on.

Similarly, if someone is taking your attention through arguments as it meets their keys of being spontaneous and special, it will cause many problems in the relationship.

It is what happened with my wife and me. We were taking each other's energy from the relationship. It became draining until we learned that we needed to give energy and changed the keys that we were using to grow the relationship.

Again, this rule applies. When you give specialness to somebody, it's a blessing when demanding and taking specialness without deserving it. Then it's a curse.

The fourth key is Storg'i, the key of love.

I know what you are thinking 'Sunny, how can love be negative?'.

Love is one of the most incredible emotions ever to experience. I 100% agree. Love is the greatest thing ever, but I'll explain the negative way to get love further down.

Positive:

It's easy to notice the positives of love.
The key of love is the key of connecting, going into each other's heart, allowing it to be opened, allowing to have that bond, that connection, that deep passion, that deep love.

When we use this key, we give love. We open our hearts up. We tell them that we love them, we allow ourselves to be vulnerable, we connect with them, we connect with family, we're open to pain and love.

When we want to allow love to enter our life, we need to open with vulnerability, which is how we form deep, meaningful connections.

The positive way to use the key of Storg'i is to give love. Appreciate the person for their kindness, caring-ness, and the small things.

Negative:

The negative way people use this key is when you manipulate people's love through dis-ingenuine comments and false actions to receive their love. Or to demand their love by continuously asking for their validation is how we take someone's love from them.

Some people can take love by being a victim and sharing all the hard times in their lives to receive love. By doing this, you are taking the energy from someone else rather than giving loving energy to another.

Another negative way love key is when we settle for a love that isn't truly who we are. We'll settle for something we believe is safe and secure rather than something we genuinely want to experience.

The Fifth key is to Surge.

Many positives come out of this. To commit to growing together within the relationship means developing a deeper meaning, a more profound sense, and deeper beliefs. You have a belief that we can get through anything together. One of the greatest beliefs that me and my wife have is that we can get through anything together. Which means whatever comes up, we can get through it. This belief is wonderful when it's at the level of the surge.

Committing to developing and being more within the relationship allows you to form a deeper bond and helps you create a conscious relationship together.

In order not to survive," I believe we should try our best at living authentically every single day because this creates a connection that lasts beyond anything else imaginable and connecting and growing together to thrive within the relationship.

We must be cautious when in a relationship to grow together. If only one partner wants to grow and the other doesn't, it could ruin the relationship. It could cause big separation within the relationship because both parties may grow apart.

The sixth key to serve:

Serving your partner's needs is one of the most special things you can do for them. To put your partner's needs before yours creates a special relationship. You create passion, deep connection, and a conscious relationship knowing your partner's needs.

One of the things you must be cautious with is doing it at your expense. It is okay to serve your partner when needed but not if it hurts your boundaries. You will need to know if they are takers and understand if they are also giving in the relationship or taking your energy.

The two keys which drive behaviours

People usually have two primary keys. These keys dictate their life and relationships. If somebody is walking around with a key of security and specialness, they will be completely different than someone that has the keys to being spontaneous and loving.

I would like you to imagine for a second, how would this be different for both people?

How would they be in relationships?

We can see that the person holding the keys of security and specialness will be looking at the world through the lens of everything that has to be safe.

If this relationship must be secure, I will need to have specific messages in the evening. I would need to know your plans, and we will have to plan far in advance, especially as you'll have to arrange something special for me and take me somewhere beautiful for me to go on this date.

From my experience, most of the problems in relationships and singles trying to find love are when they are using the keys of security and specialness.

It's our survival instinct that if I'm not the most special around, you will choose somebody else over me. Your survival instincts are looking for security and safety in the relationship.

We all have a survival brain from 2 million years ago. It's hardwired into our thinking, and it makes us think that we must survive to protect ourselves or those around us. Imagine a time when humans were hunter-gatherers. It's hard to imagine, but it was only about 2 million years ago!

In those days, our minds weren't as developed, and we had an old brain that made survival easier for us back then because of all the decisions you needed to make to survive.

When we're looking to make a relationship thrive, not survive, and to have a thriving mentality is a concept that focuses on creating a conscious relationship understanding each other's needs. When we open our relationship to thriving, the survival brain becomes obsolete.

The thoughts and opinions that were previously hardwired into us as humans can now be changed with a change in mindset. When we look at a relationship based on security and being special, we see a lot of conflict and arguments because there's only one person that could be special within a relationship at the time and certain that they are special.

I encourage looking at a relationship based on the keys of Surge and Storg'i to create a long-lasting relationship.

I will break down exactly how it helped each of these clients.

Aron had two keys that he was carrying, and the primary keys he was carrying were special and spontaneous. While he was dating, these two keys helped him in many ways.

He was very funny in relationships. He knew his worth. He was able to take ladies to the best places, to the most exceptional restaurants and help them feel connected and have a really good time.

They had a lot of fun with him because he used these two keys. However, when the relationship was to develop deeper, he would be attracting similar people to himself, which caused clashes in his relationships, arguments, and fights.

Even though his partners had the same key as him, it worked out negatively due to fight to feel special.

Having adopted a new approach, he became committed to surging within the relationship. He told me that he would adopt all six of the keys and the top two are for him to Surge and to be spontaneous within the relationship.

His dates after that became a lot better. He would always be learning about the person. The relationships had more depth, and they would plan things to grow together.

The spontaneous key kept the relationship alive, which kept him interested. He would learn about their needs and create spontaneous fun for her.

Sharon's top two keys were Security and Storg'i. With her top two keys being this, she would generally want things to be scheduled and planned.

Previously, she noticed that they identified that she would want everything to be a certain way.' I would like you to arrange a specific date. I would like you to give me enough notice.'

When things didn't go to plan, she would panic and let go of the relationship because she would try and control things, which led her to overthink.

By controlling the date, Sharon would push the good partners away. She realized that this was her issue with relationships. She had relationships in the past where sometimes she found people too boring, and that is because the person was too secure for her. They were using that key of security too much.

She decided to use all six keys, but she'd change her top two keys first. The two that she would use instead were the love of Storg'i and Surge. Surge combined with Storg'i is a powerful combination.

I asked her, by combining these, 'how would this serve your life?' She said, 'well if I get to learn and develop, I will open more, which will help my relationship grow and connect more deeply.'

Using both keys, she developed even deeper and had better relationships because this pattern of control had always held her back within relationships and friendships.

Jade had a huge realization, which helped her grow to the next level. Jade's previous keys were to serve and need security. She attracted many people who took her love, demanding to get it back, which caused a lot of conflict within her relationships.

She realized that the security she was craving was damaging her relationships, and the need to serve was another form of security. She felt trapped by valuing security so high.

She said that she needed reassurance in relationships due to the level of security she wanted, which made her seem needed.

This is the main problem with the secure attachment style, not having enough balance of spontaneousness.

Jade mentioned to me, 'Sunny, you said Serve is one of the highest keys to have in a relationship. Where did I go wrong?'

I replied: 'Serving is one of the highest needs we can meet, to serve our partners and put their needs first. It is one of the most incredible things but, when we use a key with the key to security, we're just serving constantly, not putting ourselves first, not recognizing ourselves and putting them first.'

This habitual pattern with certainty can cause issues in relationship as you will always put your partners needs first and this will meet your needs of certainty however git will be at your own determent.

The other partner could get bored. The other partner could take it because they can take it for granted. Therefore, the balance of spontaneous search and security is high.

Jade said, Sunny, I need to change mine. I'm going to commit to changing the keys to being spontaneous with relationships and of Storg'i.

This was a complete transformation for Jade that changed her habitual patterns to acknowledge and appreciate being spontaneous within the relationship. The breakthrough came with Jade when she could balance the six keys.

For you to create a passionate, loving relationship, it's about balancing all six keys out.

Task: I would like you to write down which one was your previous two primary keys?

What has this cost you in relationships?
Which two keys are you going to focus on in the future?
How would this impact your life for the rest of your relationships?

_____
_____
_____
_____
_____
_____
_____
_____
_____
_____
_____
_____
_____
_____
_____
_____
_____

Remember: Balancing the six keys and using them all in the relationships will unlock the most incredible relationship of your life. Using all the keys at once will create the most amazing relationship with passion, joy, and love.

Chapter 8

Sexual polarity

Long-term attraction is due to the sexual polarity of two people.

The law of polarity ideally means that when two forces come together, a negative and a positive, a masculine and feminine, the light and dark energy. These energies come together like magnets attracting to each other. Newton's Third Law of Motion 'For every action, there is an equal and opposite reaction'.

Sexual polarity is the opposites that create attraction and build deep connections in a relationship. The feminine and masculine sexual energy and the light and dark energy create instant attraction.

Looking for beauty only and not looking beneath the skin can cost you long-term relationships and happiness. It is becoming more common due to dating apps and social media. However, basing a relationship on this will not help you find lasting love. You will continuously find short-term relationships because sexual polarity is the difference between long-term and short-term attraction.

What is sexual polarity?

Sexual is the pull between the masculine and feminine, the opposites of each other. It is crucial to make a relationship last; it is undoubtedly the critical area for all connections to work.

Have you ever gone out to a bar or a social gathering, and someone has caught your eye, however aesthetically, they are not your type, but there is something about them? I know that's happened to me.

I went to a bar with my wife, and it was something about one of the people working there; this lady was radiant. Aesthetically she was not my type but her energy; her feminine energy was radiating and free-flowing. It drew me in like a magnet.

I told my wife that there was intrigue about her, and my wife agreed; she saw her radiance.

That is sexual polarity!

It is expected that opposites attract, which is confirmed when focusing on sexual polarity.

Opposites do attract, but not completely, as we just saw earlier in the book; the values must be aligned for the relationship to work in the long term. However, strong sexual polarity creates deep passion.

Sexual energies would need to have the polarity, the Yin and the Yang, the north and south pole.

This sexual polarity is a magnet that attracts one another.

This learning will help you rejuvenate any relationship, passion, or anything you need. When we understand that sexual energy is the key for long-term attraction, it gives you the power to create attraction any time you want to.

Reconnecting with your core sexual energy, you need to know what energy you had when you were young and free, where you are masculine, strong, decisive, or more feminine energy, open and free flowing.

Either one doesn't matter. If you're a male with feminine energy, it's okay. We want to understand what your core energy is, and this core energy is the key to attracting the right partner and allowing you to be in your essence.

A lot of female clients come to me at the start, and they speak to me and say Sunny, I want a masculine man." I look at them and think, are you a feminine woman?

Sometimes they can look feminine from the outside but internally, the energy is masculine. Therefore, they wouldn't attract a manly man as there is no polarity.

This chapter will break this down into the strategies to get into your feminine and masculine energy.

The secret is using both sexual energies is a great ability and knowing when to be in one energy and switching back to your core energy.

When we can combine masculine and feminine in different situations, we allow ourselves to be more of who we are. In contrast, if we are only super male, they may not connect with the feminine with feelings and emotions. It will limit connections and understanding of the world.

Masculine and Feminine energy!

"Ninety-nine percent of the confusion and frustration between men and women is because we assume we're versions of each other. It goes both ways, although men are a little bit more forgiving.

They allow for the mystery of women. But honestly, when men look at women, they see a softer, more lovely, multitasking, emotionally indulgent man. And they interact with us as if we're men! Realizing that we're not versions of each other meant that I needed to pay much closer attention to men than I'd originally planned."

— Alison A. Armstrong, Making Sense of Men

Appreciating the differences in sexual energy is a fundamental to creating a relationship in alignment.

Sexual Energy is different from our sex; sexual energy is the essence of who we are at the core, and what happens is for our life, we wear different masks, and these masks cover who we are due to pain or conditioning.

We wear different masks for life; if you work in a masculine environment, you will wear a masculine mask to be around work colleagues.

If your parents wanted you to be of different sex because they wanted a man within the house, they may treat you as a man, which would project a masculine mask onto you.

When we're young, we don't have the analytical parts of our brain, which means that we take the information, absorb it, and connect with it. As a result, we behave according to positive behaviour. Once you receive more love from that parent, you will take on the identity and wear the mask.

Also, later in life, you have a masculine man going to college, he hangs around with loads of females, and at that moment, he may adopt a feminine approach to fit in.

Evenly, you could be a female that works within a big corporate company, and in the masculine role, you may need to put on a male mask that will cover up who you are. But this is not the true YOU!!

It is not your true essence, and therefore it gets tiring being something you are not. We need to go back to the beginning, understand who we are about at our core, and bring out that side of us for relationships.

The divine masculine has the power to be strong, protective, loving, caring, honest, and open with emotions.

The divine feminine flourishes when feeling safe; they open up and have free-flowing energy, radiant, nurturing, caring, loving, compassionate energy.

The Divine feminine can open the masculine energy up to express. Therefore, when we get into our core sexual energy, we will now connect, love, and have a deep connection with ourselves and with our partners.

The roles of the masculine and the feminine!

The modern man may have given up many of his masculine qualities for efficiency, but an essential part remains. A faithful protector and provider - a strong provider – will always go back to the caveman days when it came down to who was needed most:

The Male energies were those offered protection from danger and entrance into society; they also provided sustenance for partners, both male & female alike.

When males were out hunting, they would need to stay quiet to ensure the prey wouldn't get away. We were conditioned to be calm and silent, in moments of suspense, and then they would attack; BOOM, they got food. Now the village is fed, and they celebrate together.

As for the females of the tribe, they will go out and collect berries and fruits. As they go out, they'll go and put their hand into the trees, and these bugs bite them.

They learned a way to be talkative, that even if they started humming or talking more, it would scare any creatures away and allow the predators to know that they are so there wouldn't be any surprise attacks.

The female brain has found a way to communicate when feeling threatened or tense. They'll show their feelings by speaking loudly and fast to let others know they may be in danger and feel fearful.

Males have different strategies; when dealing with difficult situations, males tend to stay silent and fight back, you must know what your gender does better than anybody else because there isn't much room for error on either end!

It is why a female needs to be reassured to let them know that they are safe.

Now we have differentiated the roles, and why we wear the mask of the opposite sex, it is vital to understand the key to honouring your partner's sexual energy and allowing it to shine.

The three secrets for the feminine energy to honour the masculine energy

Secret 1:

The feminine must praise the masculine.

When the masculine energy has been criticized, it's harder for them to be around that situation, stopping them from being all they can be.

There are a lot of females that criticize their partner, and once the masculine gives up, they lose all respect for them. It is crucial for a healthy relationship for the masculine energy to be praised for the way they are.

Secret 2:

The second secret to honouring the masculine energy is to allow it to be free, make decisions, take the lead, and do what it needs to do. Most partners believe that controlling the masculine energy will make the relationship better. However, it pushes them away from each other.

Secret 3:

The final secret is that feminine energy must be open; the masculine energy struggles to be around closed energy and would need to find a distraction for the situation; therefore, many men go to watch football to distract their brains from the case.

The feminine energy must be free-flowing, radiant, and open to honour the divine masculine. The open personality is like a blossoming flower that allows the masculine energy to be alive and connect.

When the feminine energy is closed off, it stops the masculine man from being himself. It limits and restricts him because the required attraction is for that feminine energy to be open, blossomed to allow the masculine to enter and be free.

The masculine energy wants to help and protect the feminine energy; however, it is difficult to defend and support the feminine when it is closed, creating conflict within the relationship.

I remember when my wife was stressed out from work and came back into the house, she went into the masculine state due to stress. She was closed off snappy and wasn't allowing me in, I would try make her laugh, to no success. I would try help her again this was shut down.

After the second day, it became uncomfortable for me, the polarity was dying down. It was very hard to be around. On the fifth day I had enough, we were arguing over small things, she would be fighting to be right and being closed minded.

That day I spoke to her and communicated how it made me feel and how it was uncomfortable for me to be around, with deeper awareness we were able to break out of that state and get back to normal.

Imagine if it had happened for five years, it would have been torture for me to live with.

The negativity would be worse, and I would be controlled and limited by the partner, complaining about everything:

'You never clean up after yourself.'

'You never take the bins'

'You always spend too much.'

All these questions start to control and limit the person.

And now, the female says,

'I don't need you.'

I would feel trapped, and he would have two choices:

1) Fight back and argue for what I believe in.

2) Step down and step into the feminine energy to balance the energy in the relationship.

Option one will make them clash and fight a lot; I may win one of the arguments or unless the approach changes or she surrenders to the masculine energy and adopts her feminine energy again.

Option two will make the female lose respect for him and any sexual attraction to the partner now, and she will start to tell herself a story of me never being the man she wanted.

She was in the opposite sexual energy due to stress and other issues, which she should have resolved to solve the problem with the relationship.

If this continued the masculine energy masculine energy that feels unwanted, not needed, no purpose within the relationship. Suddenly, will be looking for an esacpe and someone else comes into the picture, a female work colleague, and starts to work with him, connecting, seeing the masculine within him.

Praising him:

'You're really intelligent.'
'I am impressed with what you do, how did you get into it?.'

Suddenly, he feels needed from the feminine energy that laughs at his jokes, has an open personality, free-flowing energy, and is carefree. At that moment, his divine masculine is awake again at work.

He can connect with her and have the polarity once in the relationship. It may lead to an affair or the masculine planning his escape from the relationship for another one.

These feelings of being honoured for your core energy run deep into us; When someone meets your sexual energy needs, this is a hardwiring from 2 million years ago. From when we were cavemen and women, it creates a profound attraction.

Ladies, I know what you're going to be saying.

What about loyalty?

What about the other values?

I do agree.

However, there's a danger when the needs of the masculine are dismissed within the relationship, the polarity disappears, making them do crazy things. Without sexual polarity within the relationship, the chemistry will die off.

There is another option!

Option three could be for the feminine to express how she felt: I have been feeling stressed out recently with work and the bills.

I am sorry I took it out on you, let's arrange an evening together as I miss you.

This option will show the vulnerability and allow the masculine to protect and see the feminine within his partner.

The Masculine Honours The Divine Feminine

The feminine energy is breath for the masculine, allowing them to express and grow.

I like to use the example of a lioness when discussing feminine energy.

When we see the lion world, a lion must come and fight for the Lioness.

When a Lion is looking for a partner, he will approach one he likes and try to connect with her, but she will fight with him. Pushing him away, she will be testing him to see if he is strong enough.

Is he going to be there when times are hard?

The Lioness needs to understand if this partner can protect her and the family that they will create.

Now the Lion could choose to walk away; he could also lose the test with the Lioness or decide to show her that he is serious.

He will fight for the relationship and clarify that this is the partner he wants.

The Lioness needs to do this to protect her family from the Nomad Lions that come; if they try and take over the tribe and beat the male Lion, they will kill the lion cubs.

The Lion must show the Lioness their intent and commitment to protect her and be there for her. The Lioness can defend herself, but it is essential to have a partner to protect her and be there for her.

It is the most profound secret for Masculine energy when attracting feminine energy.

The first secret to honouring the feminine energy

Secret 1:

The secret is to protect her in danger, in trouble when she needs to be supported. Once the feminine feels protected by the Masculine Lion, she can express her Divine feminine core and be free.

The masculine energy must protect the feminine energy; the feminine energy is delicate and is vulnerable to hurt or criticism. It is why the masculine energy must protect the feminine, to show I am here for you.

In the olden days, feminine energy needed saving against Siberian tigers. Still, they must preserve the mother-in-law from the family, the friends ready to attack, and random people outside.

- Studies show that Four out of five women felt unsafe walking alone after dark in a park or other open space, compared to two out of five men.

It shows that it is essential to feel safe to honor the feminine energy. The masculine must form a leadership position to help the feminine energy feel safe and looked after.

Secret 2:

The masculine must notice the feminine; when the masculine sees the feminine and notices the little things, her hair, shoes, or smile. It allows her to show up in the world more; the way the feminine energy meets the needs of the masculine is by dressing up and showing her elegance to the masculine.

If it gets unnoticed, it will be a habit that stops.

Presence is the solution, giving the feminine deep presence of not focusing on anything else.

Looking deep into their eyes

Connecting with them.

Remembering all their greatness.

Secret 3:

The feminine energy must be heard!

A feminine must express the issues in their day and the problems (this isn't because they want the issue resolved). It is because they want to let it go. Being able to hear, listen, and connect with the feminine as they let go of any problems is an escape for them and helps them feel safe within the male company.

Being present is the key to hearing the feminine energy; being present is when you give them your full attention. Not focusing on other things, your phone, tv, or emails.

Giving the feminine energy 5 minutes of pure presence will create a deep, meaningful relationship.

One of my clients used to think that his partner spoke too much; this used to annoy him. Until she stopped talking to him, and this was when he knew something was up.

The feminine energy has a remarkable ability to give small details about many things, which was helpful for when we were cavemen and women as we will remember the route to get to the same destination.

The key to learning this information is appreciating the feminine world and embracing it rather than changing it.

If we think of the feminine energy like a flower, it will blossom and help create a beautiful atmosphere of love and joy when you nurture it.

A man with purpose will make women melt.

It is the main reason why when the masculine is too focused on attracting a female, they tend to move away, but when the man has a strong focus is easy for him to attract a partner.

When a man does not have a purpose, the feminine energy will be uninteresting because they think he won't provide for future family needs. Feminine energies prefer someone with an established career path who can provide for the family if needed.

A key focus for the masculine energy will be to find a purpose that will be a passion or a mission, something you would like to build for the future. Something that drives the masculine and has meaning will make you a magnet to attract the right partner.

I admire the relationship that Michelle Obama and Barack Obama have. I read that Michelle will ask Barack, what have you done today to work towards your mission to be president?

Every day, Barack Obama will have to think about the question and how he has progressed towards it. She was supporting him towards his mission.

It helped Barack be free to continue working towards his goals without guilt that he is not prioritizing her; she helped him continue his path to be more.

A surrey completed with males, in which they were asked: what is the most attractive trait in the feminine energy?

The results showed that the number one trait is;

A woman that supports their partner's dreams!

I am fortunate enough to have a partner in my life that has supported me and encouraged me to continue going to achieve my dreams since the beginning of the relationship, which allowed me to focus on building the kingdom for my family.

Once you support your partner's mission and dreams, you unlock more of the masculine partner.

https://www.endviolenceagainstwomen.org.uk/new-data-women-feel-unsafe-at-night/
— Alison A. Armstrong, Making Sense of Men - Book

I want to point out that it is evenly true that if a female's needs are not being met within the relationship and she cannot express them, is not being heard or seen.

The law of polarity will still come into play and if another person was meeting the needs of your partner than attraction will be built up.

It is important to be conscious of meeting your partners needs and creating the polarity within the relationship.

How the Yin and the Yang works for relationships!

My wife and I share similar core values to surge and love, but we have many opposite personality traits, which is key to lighting up the soul of the other partner.

A relationship is like art, a flow, a dance. In Salsa dancing, there is one lead and one that follows. It creates a polarity of movement and flow, which makes the art of dancing.

Here are some differences that we can appreciate in your future partner.

The divine feminine and the divine masculine

The light and the dark energy

Morning person and evening person

Grounded and spiritual partners

Assertive and passive

These opposites create magic to the relationship and provide a more profound passion and connection. However, the key to keeping the relationships working and the magic of love is appreciation

We see this a lot with teenagers; there is an attraction between a good girl at school and the bad boy image.

Is it because they're dangerous?
Is it because they don't care?

Yes, that's correct.

It is not the bad boy image they are attracted to; it is the bad boy's dark energy.

There is that dark energy to them. When teenagers are growing up, they have a lot of light energy to serve to be lovely to sweet as some of them need that dark energy to ignite them to be excited for the other side chemistry of the relationship.

It is vital for a combination of light and dark energy within a relationship.

This clarity of the light and dark energy is one of the most potent forces known within the relationship, this force of the light and dark creates a high level of passion and excitement.

THE SEXY ELEMENT

DARK SWEET SPOT LIGHT

The light energy:	The Dark energy
Playful	Assertive
Loyal	Direct
Sweet	Bold
Caring	Selfish (within the relationship)
Considerate	Strong
Putting others first	Risk-taker
Serving	Rulebreaker
Shy	Wild

The selfishness of the dark energy knows what they want.

I want you
No one else matters
Making them the priority
It is creating time for each other and ignoring others.

The light energy will want to attend the family get-together and keep the family happy, while the dark energy is okay to break the rules.

That light energy can light up souls with their caring, loving energy while the dark energy can let the light energy have balance, to not over care about others, and when two souls and two powers come together in the form of the Yin and the yang, the dark and the light.

If you have always been in light energy and the person you are also speaking with is light energy, it may not create the depth needed to take the relationship to the next level.

As you create the dark energy within the relationship by being more direct with flirting and more honest, it will add the spice the relationship needs to progress things.

Showing the light energy that you have dark energy within allows you to move the relationship to the next level.

We need to evoke the darkness within us.

Instead of being polite when getting to know a partner, you can be more direct and see what happens.

If they are dark energy, you can utilize your playful light energy to grow the relationship.

I want you to know that all you need is within you.

You are the creator of your relationships, and you can create the intimacy you desire.

To get back into your masculine state tips.

Meet other males

Go take up kickboxing or martial art class.

Go to the gym lifting heavyweights.

How to get into feminine state tips:

Dance free-flowing dancing - connecting with your body

Go to get your hair done/ nails

Have a girl's night

Using the words, 'I feel' is a powerful way to connect with yourself.

What sexual mask have you been wearing in previous relationships?

What will you do to ensure that you stay in your core sexual energy?

_____

_____

_____

_____

_____

Task:

I would like you to write down some habits that you can take up to get you back into your core energy.

_____

_____

_____

Aron implemented this information in the following way:

Aron was a very masculine male, and he liked independent females, which he didn't need to protect or look after; he didn't want females that needed him.

It made him attract the wrong partner based on his level of polarity. When you are highly masculine, it will draw in feminine women, but by understanding the keys to allow the feminine to be free, he realized that he could protect and be present with the feminine whilst giving them to be free.

It helped him to develop deeper relationships with females as he was able to understand their needs.

Sharon went through a difficult childhood which led her to protect herself as she couldn't trust anyone, which means that she covered up her divine feminine energy. It was a way to protect her from future heartbreak and pain.

It was tiring for Sharon as she had a beautiful feminine core when she was young, and it was circumstances that led her to stop being free and express herself.

She would try and make all the decisions within relationships; she would try and control situations when dating. In relationships, she struggled to praise males because she didn't respect them. These factors were pushing the divine masculine out of her life.

Sharon could not surrender to the divine masculine energy to allow them to take the lead and be comfortable with the uncomfortable.

She didn't allow herself to be protected by anyone as she thought it was a weakness. It was realizing that masculine energy would always be there when she needed it allowed her to become more open to allowing the divine feminine to come out and create an opening for a masculine partner to enter.

It is essential to understand that there can only be one masculine partner in a relationship at a time; I know many of you are thinking, what about homosexual relationships?

Well, think about this, when you see homosexual relationships, you usually see a butch partner (masculine) and a softer partner (feminine).

The law of polarity always works for attraction.

After doing more profound healing work with Sharon, she was able to bring out the feminine side, knowing that the masculine side is always there if she needed it to step in.

Sharon had to surrender her need for control and her need to be correct. To truly appreciate and praise the masculine energy.

Jade uses this information very beautifully; Jade had very open and beautiful energy within a relationship. She was very free-flowing and open in relationships. However, Jade didn't praise men since her ex-partner and became closed off around the masculine. She knew that this was pushing the masculine man away from what she wanted in her life.

She committed to giving up her need for control within situations and relationships, allowing the masculine energy to feel free and strong.

I have created a meditation for you to complete to connect you with your core sexual energy; it will reprogram the key things you need to learn about relationships and your sexual energy.

Appreciation

The critical factor here comes from appreciating your partner's differences. When you first meet someone and tell you something new about them, we are curious about what makes them unique.

It interests you because you appreciate the differences within them. They create a variety within the relationship.

After spending more time together and becoming more familiar with each other, the differences become issues, the difference in view becomes challenges, and the uniqueness becomes irritating. The appreciation has disappeared due to arguments, expectations, and fear.

If we keep the same appreciation from the start, we will keep the same magic till the end.

My wife and I always joke around about this.

We always talk about how she's a morning person; in the morning, she talks, always having energy, wide awake, and she brings so much excitement to the daytime. I am the complete opposite in the morning though, and I am quiet; it takes me a long time to get into my flow.

I need a good 45 minutes of meditation mindset right for the day, and then I can come alive. Then in the evening, the roles reverse.

I am loud

I am full of energy
And I share my energy with her.

It is as if we both work in different time zones, and because I appreciate her morning gifts, it will add value to me, and I will be able to add value in the evening.

This contrast allows us to be more of ourselves and experience more of life. For example, imagine if we were both morning people waking up full of energy and both tired at night-time, we will both be bored during the evenings. Some may say that is perfect, which it could be for some people, but we both value being spontaneous in our relationship therefore, we appreciate the excitement we both bring to the relationship.

Another factor is my wife is a talker, and I'm a thinker.

When I think things through, she is already saying them out loud because I appreciate the polarity; I can enjoy being around her and find it funny when she expresses it out loud first.

Imagine if we were both thinkers, none of us would speak in the relationship, which may lead to us becoming bored.

When you can appreciate the other person's gifts, it can create a beautiful relationship.

When I was young, I believed that everyone should be like how you are, and one of the critical things that we like is people like us or how we want to be.

Sometimes a partner will come into your life to bring out a different side of you, a part of you that needed to come out.

Being open to this will allow you to look at relationships through a new pair of eyes.

When someone comes into your life, it brings out a different part of you, heals you, or helps you grow. We usually resist things that we need to lean into to get learnings or create a better life.

A Stanislav Grof M.D. is a psychiatrist with over sixty years of experience researching non-ordinary states of consciousness. He believed that the emotions in life are aligned and there for a purpose. When we are triggered by emotions of others or realising emotions within, it is essential to investigate them to discover what we need to learn to evolve in life.

It is also similar in relationships; if we are strongly resisting a trait of somebody, we must ask ourselves, what is triggering, what is the frustration with their actions.

Are their parts of myself unhealed?

When we try to resist it, and we have some resentment in someone else, it's something inside of us that's showing up.

Even if you meet someone you don't like, it is good to understand why you feel nasty towards them and heal it within yourself.

When I first met my wife, she would laugh so much. And she would laugh over the minor things.

In the past, laughing had to be over something special; it had to be a funny joke or an event or something like that.

I would think, what was funny? At the time, I was in corporate finance and had a severe outlook on life; she was able to share a gift of laughter within me and made me let go of the serious side that kept coming up.

Now I'm starting to laugh at the smallest of things. I was resisting at first, but it was what I needed. Imagine from corporate finance to love coaching; I had to evolve through that process. I had to step out of what I thought was my ordinary and structured world to be more open to change.

It is like each season changes spring to summer, summer to autumn, autumn to winter, and winters to spring again. Just as each of these seasons change, we can follow.

Perhaps one day, we need to show that the other side of us is here in the relationship. The side for spontaneity, love, security, surge, and sharing different parts of us will allow us to experience more life.

Task:
I would like you to list critical differences that you appreciate with your friends and family and notice how their differences allow you to bring out a different side within you…

_____

_____

_____

_____

_____

_____

_____

The transition period between the male and female

Arguments used to occur due to minor things that
happened.

Have you ever found that the minor thing can create an
argument in the past?

The transition period could be the reason why!!

Understanding masculine and feminine energy are crucial
and co-creating together comes down to transition.

A transition period is different between the masculine and
the feminine energy; the transition period is once you have
completed one task, how quickly can you move on to
another?

The masculine energy will need to have a 5/10-minute
transition period from one task to another, from work to
home. The male brain needs to digest and precisely
understand what is required from them in the situation;
once it approaches another position, it needs to recap once
again, which causes a delay in reaction.

The female brain doesn't need any transition period due to
diffused awareness that a female has, which can use
different brain parts to be more aware and help them
understand more than one thing at once.

The key to understanding the transition period is to give
the masculine brain space to breathe between events. When
the male mind returned from work, it would need a period
to switch off and focus on the relationship again.

My wife used always to discuss this at deep levels. We'll go out to an event as we return; my mind is still transitioning from the event to all the great things we saw.

Coming back to normality takes longer for the male brain to digest everything. I just had to digest the information and then become cantered on it to be present again in the relationship. However, as my wife has a feminine brain, she would be looking at me expecting me to do multiple things simultaneously, as the feminine brain can do due to diffused awareness.

She would look at me and ask, what are you thinking?

What's the problem?

Is something a problem with the relationship?

I would say I'm lovely. There's no issue, but my wife wouldn't believe it as she never knew that there were different transition periods for the male and female brains.

Once we both learned about this, we understood that both minds take a more extended processing system to digest and change the environment, which helps us understand each other's world.

How do you think this can impact your connection to the opposite sexual energy?

_____

_____

_____

_____

Chapter 9

Communication

The level of your communication will reflect your relationships

What is the best way to communicate with your future partner?

This chapter will give you the skills to not be hurt and connect with a partner at a deep level to build rapport and connection.

We now have all the skills and the ability to be great communicators.

We have made massive internal shifts going from anxious/avoidant to secure, stepping into our higher selves as the King and Queen. We now want to communicate with a potential partner, and it is vital to understand the best way to do this.

The essence to communication is understanding, clarifying, and seeing the other persons perception.

I'm going to share strategies here for you to use directly with people you are meeting and people you're connecting with.

I need you to understand that there are only two forms of communication.
1) A cry for help.
2) A loving response.

All forms of communication fall under these two headings. If somebody is being rude and bad-mannered, it is a cry for help. If they're trying to cut you off, trying to prove a point, trying to belittle you, if they're saying why they're not good enough, then these are all cries for help.

A loving response is where you're empowering, supporting, caring, being funny, lifting the energy. Let's be clear on what we need.

It seems like people are being hurt right now in dating, and they're using the wrong approach with it. It is forgotten that most people on dating apps want a relationship however, they are unable to communicate what they really want!

Men, if you're sending nude pictures or demanding weird pictures straight away, it's obviously a cry for help because you have self-doubts about yourself. Therefore, you're trying to gain your acceptance by receiving a personal image of someone.

We know that it puts females off, leading with sexual images will damage your reputation and show that you are only good for S E X! I trust that the people sending nudes have more to offer than their bodies. I hope you can realise this as well.

Some females are also direct and sexual. They are both cries for help. I want us to view it this way for you not to take it personally when communicating with a potential partner.

How can we communicate in the right way to create a deeper connection, and how can leading with a loving response resolve many communication issues?

Now for every form of communication, there's a strategy that we can follow that will help us along the way. The strategy I'm going to share with you is the FBI technique and Neuro-Linguistic Programming. This is called matching and mirroring.

Mirroring and Matching

Mirroring and matching are the best way to build quick rapport with another person. It is a natural way that two people form a deep connection because we like people that are like ourselves.

It is a subconscious way of saying that you are like me, and I am safe.

When you mirror or match somebody, it shows that you are interested in them, that you want to get to know them better, and it also makes them feel comfortable with you.

By doing this, it will help the communication process to flow. The benefits of mirroring and matching are that it helps build trust, improves communication, and can help to resolve conflicts.

When you're in a conversation with somebody, you want to make sure that you match them physically, emotionally, and verbally.

Physically means that you're sitting or standing in the same position as them, you're using the same gestures, and your body is facing in the same direction.

Emotionally means that you're mirroring their facial expressions; if they smile, you smile; if they frown, you frown. You're also mirroring their vocal tonality; if they speak softly, you speak softly, and if they speak loudly, you speak loudly.

Verbally means that you're using the same words as them. Mirroring people and matching their body language is a great way to build rapport and connect with them emotionally. I like adding in what they're saying by reflecting it back to them. This will show you care about the person while also letting them know that everything said has been heard clearly.

Pacing during conversations involves using the same level of tone as the other person, which can help create a connection. Once you are in rapport, you will lead the conversation and communication.

Leading helps you go deeper into conversations and steer the conversation in the direction you would like, to connect deeper.

Have you ever had a friend that you automatically connect with when you break it down;
Do you speak similarly?
Do you speak a similar tone, pace, volume?
Do you have similar hand gestures?
Do you have a similar movement?

I would like you to notice the next time you are with a friend to see if you naturally create similar movements or use similar words.

We like people that are just like us or how we want to be. That's why matching, and mirroring is very powerful.

The different ways that we can match are:
Body movement
Language
Words that they say
Breathing
Beliefs
Vision
Laughter
Eye contact
Timing of messages
Intensity
Energy

The deepest level of communication and matching is that if you can match the other person's energy, it creates an incredible, more profound bond than what we can see.

If you are in joy and you meet someone who has the same energy as you, it helps you create a higher vibration of energy together. Just look at sports crowds as they celebrate together. They can connect deeper.

Quantum physics has shown that atoms that vibrate at the same level bond together. Looking deeper into this, if you vibrate at the same level as another person energetically, you will automatically bond together. In contrast, if they had a different level of frequency, it would be harder to connect.

Has this happened in your life before, where you've moved away from somebody, and you didn't know why? Or maybe they were moaning too much. So, you take a step away. Now that we're aware of it, we can change it.

When you see someone sharing positive information or lifting the mood, they give a loving response and share a high vibration of communication. If someone pulls your energy down, they are likely crying for help.

I would like you to be aware of the language you share with the world and partners.

If someone says all men are terrible - this is a cry for help. If someone says I'm excited for all the potential partners, I could meet online - this is a loving response.

If someone says you are ugly - this is a cry for help. I want to sleep with you - this is a cry for help.

I want to take you somewhere amazing - this is a loving response.

We connect with people through the conversation that we share. If you were to share a cry for help, you would be met with another cry for help.

Now, I would like you to think of how having a communication style of love will impact your life?

If you were to communicate with loving responses, it is more likely that you will connect with more people that share loving responses. Sharing information from a grateful place and being vulnerable and open about yourself, is a fantastic place to start.

As we looked at previously, who do you want to attract in the world, and how would they speak?

Would they be positive, negative, joyful, fun, loving?

Based on the person you want to attract; how should you communicate?

If you are looking for someone ambitious, you must share your goals and the books you read. If you want someone into health, share your health journey, the foods you eat, the yoga you do, etc. This will make them interested in your life.

The rules of polarity still count while communicating. Polarity is teasing or expressing your thought process, even if it differs from theirs. It is vital to have aligned values and having different views of life can help create deeper conversations.

Remember: Mirroring and matching are for rapport. Once you have rapport, you want to share more about yourself and create the depth of a relationship through communication.

Here's what I mean. Have you ever been in an argument with somebody, and they try to be cheeky and tell a joke, but it frustrates you?

Yeah, that's because you're not in rapport with each other. So, there must be rapport, matching, and mirroring for all change and influence to happen.

Knowing which key is the most important to you and the partner you want will enable you to have deeper conversations by using the keys.

Security communication:
How are you?
How was your day?

Spontaneous communication:
Where would you like to travel to? I am planning my next trip away.
I was thinking of you, how are you?

Special communication:
I was thinking about how amazing you are. You drive me crazy!
My day was busy. I have had business meetings nonstop, and I love it.

Strong communication:
I spent the day relaxing with my family and connecting with everyone I love! How are you?
Tell me a story from when you were young?

Surge communication:

I have been reading this fantastic book; this is what I got from it. What are you reading?
Who is your role model?

Serve communication:

Giving pure presence to your partner and listening, asking deeper questions, and giving the time to understand them without judging or interrupting.

How we receive communication

I'm going to break down here the NLP communication model. It says that the world that we see outside is represented and internalized within our minds. These internal representations within our mind are based on our values, experiences, and the past.

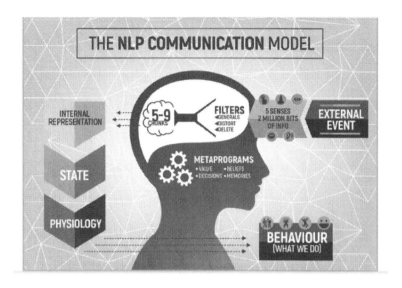

When we bring in information, we filter it to help us understand it faster; this is done by generalizing and deleting information. When we generalize, it is based on matching it to behaviour we recognize from the past. The reason why the mind does this is that we're taking in vast amount of information at once.

Sometimes we misunderstand the information and link it to the past, even if there is no relationship with the behaviours It is essential to understand as our assumptions can be incorrect and trigger a painful past event in the mind that causes us to close off.

Sometimes somebody can ask for a photo, and automatically we're assuming it's a naughty suggestion because of an experience. This is how the brain filtering system works because of the emotional triggers.

The solution is to be in the right state before communicating and understand what is triggered inside you if you feel annoyed or disrespected when speaking with a potential partner.

Now, close your eyes.

Take some deep breaths inwards and focus your attention on your heart.

I want you to find that Queen or King within.

If you have any blocks, I would like to inhale and let them go.

If you're feeling anxious about talking to a person.

I need you to remind yourself that you are enough.

I need you to give yourself love.

Accept yourself.

Then, when you feel recharged to your higher self, I want you to text or message or call and connect with your potential partner.

Following this technique will ensure that you show up to the world as your highest self and create meaningful conversations.

Now that we've spoken about the two main ways of communication and our internal representation that brings in information.

Here are potential responses when communicating with others.

You must develop the skills to communicate within. I will give you some examples; however, the key to communication is authenticity.

I will give you some examples of great responses and great ways to get people's attention. I want you to have the power to create them yourself.

I would like for you to think of 4 different emotional responses.

An angry response
A courageous response
A loving response
and a fearful response

Now, if somebody messaged you on a dating site, saying, 'when was the last time you were in a relationship'?

How would you deliver a fearful response?

Well, it would probably go something like, 'oh, no, he doesn't want to date me because I haven't been in a relationship for a long time'.

And you may not reply to him.

Or you may send him a message to say it doesn't matter.

You may come across as rude.

And by doing that, you're going to disconnect from the relationship.

'An angry response could be, why do all men and women ask stupid questions'?

'I hate this question'.

A courageous response could be open and honest:

'It's been a few years where I've been working on myself and building who I am to find the right person'.

Or a loving response could be:

'I've always met the wrong ones, but now I'm here ready to meet the right person when they come along'.

I know that sounds a bit cheesy, but sometimes the cheese is needed.

I need you to realize that you always have a decision. You always have a choice.

How you feel, how you think, and how you create.

How you respond is always in your control.

Even if somebody is rude, you can never give your power away. By letting them take over your emotional state, they get to own your energy by being rude to you.

That means they will win.

Imagine somebody has given you a gift and this gift has a smell, and doesn't look nice.

Now you have this smelly object that you dislike in your house. You're going to feel disgusted. You're going to think, what do I do with this.

It is going to lower your energy.

Now imagine they tried to give you the gift and you said 'No, thank you'. That person will keep the disliked gift.

If someone tries to be rude to you and you don't accept it, they suffer.

We don't need to accept all the messages and the rudeness of another person.

A great way of communicating with a potential partner is to express how you feel. If they were rude, you could express this to them.

Another method of communication is telling stories about yourself to help them understand who you are. You can share stories of your core values and explain how you live by your values.

Boundaries make relationships work

Boundaries are when you set clear communication of what you will tolerate within a relationship.

When there is a lack of boundaries within a relationship, it can often lead to resentment, anger, and frustration. When it comes to dating, it's essential to establish what your boundaries are early on. This way, there is clarity and expectations for both parties involved.

A relationship without boundaries causes chaos as there is no clear standard of what to expect.

When we set a boundary, it signifies personal respect and courage. This helps your partner see your worth. A boundary is something that needs to be respected by you and your partner.

I struggled to set boundaries in the past, and personal relationships were pulling too much of my energy without me being aware. It affected my individual needs, time, and energy and damaged me.

I wouldn't be able to show up to the world the way I wanted to because of a relationship pulling me down.

When I started to set boundaries within relationships, it was difficult as people already had an expectation of how I would be. Therefore, it is essential to set a boundary early.

Sticking to your boundaries is crucial to demonstrate self-respect and what you will tolerate within a relationship. A boundary is moving the relationship to the next level. An example of a boundary is going exclusive and not speaking to other people.

When you set a boundary with somebody that is narcissistic and controlling, they run away because they don't respect boundaries and other people's requests. This allows you to not suffer in a controlling relationship.

Now that you have built your house and identity of power, and had affirmations engraved, empowering habits and beliefs to become this secure Queen or King. You need to be aware of who you are letting into your house; if someone takes your energy or pulls you down, you will need to set boundaries of what you will or will not tolerate.

It is a must to set clear boundaries for your future. If you tolerate disrespect early on, you will always tolerate it within the relationship. If you can stop it early, it will be beneficial. It will allow you to set a new standard within the relationship, one of love, joy, and a higher level of communication and connection.

By setting boundaries, you will be an inspiration to your children and grandchildren as they will be able to set them as well.

I know you can do it!

And I know that the person going to date you will value you even more because of it, the right person that will come into your life, will value you because of you.

Remember, mindful living is about being selective with the thoughts that go through your head. You can't let other people's beliefs or unhelpful emotions have space in this precious being called "you." Be mindful and respect yourself, so you don't give room for anything less than what serves YOU best!

Chapter: 10

Know what you want

This section will be among the most impactful for you. It will cover selecting your ideal partner, who you want as your partner, and how you'd like your partner to add to your life. I believe that the person that we choose to be in a relationship with is among, or, if not, the most important decision that we can make in our life, especially when we consider long-term relationships.

The decision as to who you decide to spend your life is of profound importance. Here are a couple of key things you should consider when searching for your soulmate to finally awaken the lover within.

Proximity

Proximity carries an essential role in relationships. Countless times, couples have engaged in long-distance relationships, only to end it shortly. In the long term, difficulties arise in terms of the overall chemistry, which slowly begins to vanish.

We have all heard of a situation where you're working with somebody, and they start getting close, one thing leads to another, and they begin to form a relationship or even an affair. This is mainly because chemistry is brought about via proximity, and your closeness to your potential partner is crucial in making the relationship work.

Therefore, always ensure that the partner you're looking for is somebody close by and somebody you can see often.

Selection

Selection is what helps us choose a partner with whom we'd like to engage in a long-term relationship, as opposed to choosing someone who's looking for something more short-term.

Many of us are generally unaware of the keys to selection. Psychological studies show that human beings are usually attracted to those who fill the void we have in our lives or are emotionally unavailable.

We would want somebody to fill the missing gap from childhood to prove that we can have the love we never received.

More specifically, if the love you craved the most as a child was an absent father, you will subconsciously attract someone more absent from filling the void and receiving the love you never received. It can cause issues in your life by choosing the wrong partner continuously as you try and fill the gap rather than choosing a life partner.

The wounds from your childhood may seem like they're healing; however, it's important to recognize this as sabotaging your journey.

As stated earlier in the book, it's through inner healing and inner love which we can let go of these problems. Once you understand this, you have the power to bring the right person into your life and truly embark on a beautiful love journey.

Think, Believe, Manifest

I'd like you now to visualize, think abundant thoughts, and dream limitlessly of your desired partner. Keep your fears at bay, and don't hold back.

Some of you may currently be visualizing your soulmate. Some of you may be experiencing doubtful thoughts along the lines of: Am I asking for too much? What if nothing happens?

These thoughts are understandable, but what if the signs of manifesting your dream partner were always there? For example, you may be familiar with the quote "ask, and you shall receive." You may also be familiar with a concept known as the law of attraction, which further expands on the idea that your thoughts can become manifested, and Oprah Winfrey and Tony Robbins endorse this concept.

The law of attraction has played a phenomenal role in understanding how to expand our consciousness and manifest our dream partners.

When manifesting their dream partners, practitioners commonly use the law of attraction to write down a list comprising their dream partner's key traits.

I believe that having a list can be of profound help, and we'll dwell on the reason why in a moment. However, your list needs to carry these key attributes and have clarity because an ambiguous list of traits may invite the wrong person into your life.

"I am the master of my fate."

The reticular activating system is an antenna inside the mind that can help you attract what you focus on. The powerful thoughts we emit to the universe. Whether we realize this or not, is constantly influencing our lives. Here's one of my most memorable manifestations.

Recently, I'd been looking to purchase a Tesla, which was on my vision board. I'd test-driven a model that I liked and fell in love with the car. It was all I could think of, from the moment I woke to the second I'd fall asleep.

Suddenly, with my brain constantly emitting thoughts of this car, I noticed Tesla's everywhere! Every time I would drive, I would see a Tesla.

Coincidence?

Perhaps Tesla's were simply growing more popular? However, scientific studies indicate that when we have excessive thoughts about a particular thing, we shut these thoughts within our mind and become fixated on them, to the extent that when this thing appears, we notice it rapidly and more frequently. I encountered many Tesla's in this scenario because it was my mind's primary focus.

Now, I'd like to ask our female readers to recall if there was a time in which you purchased a beautiful, eye-catching dress, and shortly after, when attending a party, you quickly noticed somebody wearing the same dress. I'm sure this has happened before, right? This is among the few examples of manifesting things every day.

Tony Robbins perfectly summarizes the concept of manifestation as follows: "Where focus goes, energy flows."

I want to show you how this technique is often applied to dating. People looking for a partner tend to dwell on the type of partner they don't want, rather than the type of partner with the traits they are looking for. However, the universe cannot distinguish between what we want and don't want within our partner.

If you tell the universe, "I don't want someone who lies," all the universe hears is a liar. If you tell the universe, "I don't want someone that cheats," then the universe will send somebody unfaithful because it cannot distinguish between someone unfaithful and *not* unfaithful.

I remember recently working with one of my clients on this issue. As I spoke with her, we discussed what she was looking for in her dream partner, and as she told me, she mentioned she didn't want a liar, didn't want someone dishonest, or someone who would hurt her. I told her that to find her dream partner; you must focus solely on what you want.

She said, "Sunny, that's too difficult. Because all I know is what I don't want."

For the first part of this exercise, I would like you to start by writing down in the table below 20 things that you don't want in your partner. This could be dishonesty, unfaithfulness, aggressiveness, selfishness.

Whatever comes to mind. I encourage you to get creative.

_____

_____

_____

_____

_____

_____

_____

_____

_____

_____

_____

_____

_____

_____

_____

_____

_____

_____

_____

_____

_____

_____

_____

_____

_____

Well done. That must feel good to write down all the things you don't want. Some of you may find it easier to write this down than the next exercise.

When considering what we want, it is essential to know the type of relationship you would like to develop:

Three stages to relationships.

Stage 1	Macho Male	Submissive Female
Stage 2	Independent Male	Independent Female
Stage 3	Conscious Warrior	Full Goddess

Stage one is when we have a masculine macho relationship with a very feminine woman.

Stage 1 shows a patriotic relationship.

When the masculine man provides financially and looks after the family, he would have the final say in the house, and the women would typically take the lead of the family house activities. The female is dependent on the male in this relationship this is viewed as an old-school relationship approach.

The second stage relationship shows a balanced relationship.

In recent years, we have evolved our relationships with each other. Stage two is when the female is working and is financially independent, she has a good education and can depend on herself. The male also is financially stable and educated. Now we have two independent people living together, coexisting together, and living a life together.

During this period, they formed good roommates but never created the sexual polarity they wished to have within the relationship. They are stuck in this stage and unable to

194

have the deep connection and passion they want as the roles are unclear.

We can see that the stage 2 relationship offers a more significant relationship than stage one because there isn't one submissive person being limited by the other.

The stage 2 relationship has limitations because maintaining the sexual polarity is an issue with this level of relationship. Partners in a stage 2 relationship may start to see each other as equal, and they could begin to match the effort each of them puts into the relationship.

This level of thinking will create divides in the relationship and cause separation as they count what each partner contributes to the relationship.

And now is the time to evolve to the third stage.

Now is the time for us to go to the next part of our journey.

The third stage relationship is of the highest evolution.

This is what I call a conscious warrior and a flourished goddess.

The third stage male is a conscious warrior, somebody who is strong, has started his journey on the healing process, to become more and not to let the past hold back. To be protective, caring, loving, to see his partner, understand her, and to connect with her and understand her needs.

The third stage female is a flourished goddess, strong, intelligent, powerful, independent but wants a partner.

Someone who is beautiful and knows her worth can have compassion, love, and surrender to the masculine presence.

She's able to praise her partner. She can allow him to lead the relationship and give him the freedom he needs to grow.

After my client let go of what she didn't want, it was simple. She wanted all the things opposite to that. Instead of somebody that was a cheat, she wanted someone loyal.

Someone that is:
Kind, considerate, caring, family-oriented, protective, loving, spiritual.

Now that she started focusing on what she wanted within a relationship, she started seeing more of these people and noticed that there were great people out there.

That's exactly what I need you to do.
It's time to focus on all the great men and women out there. What traits do they have that you like?

Maybe you have a friend, business partner, colleague, or someone you've seen on TV, or they're famous, and you like their traits?

Personally, for me, I love the traits of Michelle Obama. She is a strong woman who can connect with people and empower her husband. These are exceptional traits that you want in a female.

Now imagine the right partner coming into your life. How would they be?

What are some of the traits they will have?

Will they be attractive, caring, loving, masculine, feminine?

Write down 20 of the traits and characteristics that you like. And I'm telling you to be specific.

One of my clients was clear on this. He wrote down everything he wanted, and this woman came into his life six weeks later. He said to me, 'Sunny, she isn't as tall as I wanted'.

I asked him, did you write this down on your list? And he replied, saying 'No, I never'. It wasn't a deal-breaker, but it is good to be clear of what you want.

Now it is your time to write down what you want in your partner?

Example: caring, loving, considerate, family orientated, strong, inspirational, protective, nurturing, funny, witty, sexual, passionate, etc.

_____

_____

_____

_____

_____

_____

_____

_____

_____

_____

_____

_____

_____

_____

_____

_____

_____

_____

_____

_____

_____

_____

_____

_____

_____

_____

_____

_____

_____

Amazing! Now we are clear on the person we want.

I would like you to rank them in order of importance to be clear on what matters the most to you.

Now, I would like you to consider a few questions I will be asking and see which one excites you as to what you want in a partner.

How do you feel to have this person come into your life and connect with you?

Start thinking about what life would be like together. What are the amazing things that you will both do?

Would you like to travel the world?
Spend some nice family time connecting and enriching your life to a higher level?
Would you go to spiritual events together?
Would you go to personal development events?
Would you both come to one of my future events?
To connect and to go deeper within your relationship?
How would you like your relationship to be romantic?
Or would you like it to be with a lot of humour?

How would it feel to have this partner in your life?
How would it feel for this partner to love you
unconditionally?

To recognize the beauty within you to appreciate all of you.

How would that make you feel?
How do you connect? How do you kiss?
And how would you feel having that partner in your life?
Would you do salsa together?

Write it down below in as much detail as possible:

_____
_____
_____
_____
_____
_____
_____
_____
_____
_____
_____
_____
_____

Remember, being clear on what you want will help you
realize what you will not tolerate within a relationship; this
helps create your personal red flags and green flags.

A few years ago, I went through a similar process at a seminar and designed exactly what I wanted within a partner. I wrote down everything essential for me to be in a happy relationship.

As I became aware of this, I would notice the key things that were missing from my relationship, and I would focus on this, creating a more significant issue.

I was focused on her becoming a queen, being this amazing person, and being passionate.

Our relationship had passion, connection, love, and intimacy, but I was focused on the one small thing that was missing at the time. I wanted her to be a queen, to show up strong and elegant. I wanted this beautiful woman to be passionate, caring, loving, and at the highest level.

I wanted the most profound connection. I was annoyed when I realized she wasn't all these things. But something dawned on me. I wasn't either.

I was playing as a joker.
I was playing at a low level.
I wasn't showing up to the relationship like a King.

I wasn't as passionate, playful, appreciating her beauty, being strong for her, being funny, connecting with her, giving her presence.

I was the problem that was creating the problem within the relationship.

Who do you need to be to have this fulfilling, loving relationship?

I would like you to look deep down inside and see who you need to become to create this relationship?

Who do you need to be?

More strong, confident, calm, secure, open-hearted, assertive, empathetic, look after yourself, work out, healthier, dress smarter, learn more, believe more in yourself, more masculine, more feminine, the King, the Queen.

Do you need to be more open?

Less judgmental?

Who do you need to be to attract this person in your life?

How do you need to show up to the world to a vibrational frequency match, so you can both connect at the same level?

It's important that we make a vibrational match. If we do not, then the relationship will not last.

An interesting statistic is that 70% of lottery winners go broke. They do not have the wealth foundations and principles to maintain the money. They are missing the abundance vibration and knowledge, which makes them lose money.

It is important that you are clear on the person you must be to maintain the relationship you want.

Who do you need to be to attract your partner? List 20 things below.

_____

_____

_____

_____

_____

_____

_____

_____

_____

_____

_____

_____

_____

_____

_____

_____

_____

_____

_____

_____

_____

_____

_____

_____

_____

_____

_____

_____

_____

_____

_____

I would like you to highlight the ones you need to work on the most.

Now we have a map of what is needed to bring in the partner you want.

Being clear on who you are and who you want your partner to be will create a vibrational match to attract the right partner into your life.

Your Why!

The Stronger Your Why, The Greater the Results.

What's the purpose behind creating a beautiful, passionate relationship?

I remember when I discovered my reason, the reason I wanted to create a beautiful relationship with my partner, it brought me to tears.

I always thought it was because I wanted to be happy, but when I went deeper, I realized it was because I wanted to be the father to my children that I never had, and I wanted to be someone with integrity, compassion, kindness, and joy.

This exercise is powerful because it overcomes the smaller obstacles in your pursuit of love when you dig deeper.

Another client completed this exercise, and her why became so deep-rooted that it triggered an emotional response.

She wanted to be the generational change for her family. She would change the way women would be treated in her family in the future.

Now I will ask you:

What is the goal? What is the relationship you want to create?

_____

_____

_____

And why is this important to you?

_____

_____

_____

And why is that important to you? (Go deeper)

_____

_____

_____

_____

And why is that important to you? (Go deeper into the last answer)

_____

_____

_____

And honestly, why is that important to you? (Go even deeper)

_____

_____

_____

And why is that so important to you? (What would it do for others)

_____

_____

_____

And why is that important to you? (Keep going deeper)

_____

_____

_____

Finally, why is that important to you?

_____

_____

_____

_____

My client wanted to create a fantastic, passionate, loving relationship. At first, I asked, why is it essential for you to create this?

She said because I want to be happy. And I want love in my life.

When I asked her, why is that important for you?

She said 'it's important to me because I never had love in my life when I was younger. I want love in my life now'.

And I asked, why is that important to you?

It is because I deserve love; I want love in my life. I also want to give love to others.

When I asked why it is that important for you to give love to others?

She said she wants to give love and fulfilment, to help someone else, and show her children the image of how love should be and how it feels to be loved.

Why is that important to you?

Because she didn't want her children to have her life, she wanted to be a role model for generations.

When asked why is that important to you?

She said 'My family didn't have the proper guidance and support needed. Therefore, I want to show how much love I can give and how much love the child truly deserves. She doesn't want her children to go through the same problems'.

Her reason was more significant than any of these scary dating stories, and her motivation was to change her love destiny for her children to see a better life.

Now this woman was ready to create the love she wanted in her life as she was so clear on why.

It is what I want all of us to do and ensure it's very clear. I would love you to post it on to the group.

https://linktr.ee/sunnysekhon

And show the world the relationship that you are committed to creating.

Now the final steps are an action plan to create it. You know who you must be. Now it's time to execute and get yourself out there.

Where would your ideal partner be?

Set up a 4-week plan of how you are going to meet your partner?

Will it be on dating apps, work, coffee shops, events, gym, dating events, etc?

_____

_____

_____

_____

_____

_____

_____

_____

Chapter: 11

Dating Apps

Dating app are one of many ways to attract the right partner.

The most important thing is you want to be showing your best self, and you want to be putting your best foot forward.

Think of it as if you were at a job interview, you show up as the best version of yourself, and this is the same with dating apps. It is essential to show the best side and share about yourself.

I want you to understand and appreciate that we all have our weaknesses.

Initially, we want to build that attraction; connecting and being vulnerable is essential to make a more profound connection with your potential partner. When you are only sharing superficially, it costs you time and the ability to get to know someone honestly.

If you want to attract somebody smart and into business, you will also need to show a nice, classy, elegant look. If you're going to attract an intelligent female, you must also show your intelligence, and you must wear something that expresses your intellect.

You can't be wearing joggers and a jumper if you're trying to find somebody that's smart, intelligent, professional. There will be an image mismatch, and we are attracted to people like us.

We must remember dating apps are initially superficial. When we look deeper into them, they are a fantastic tool to connect with people, like social media. It provides a vast amount of information about someone. You can understand if they smoke, have children, are married, or have religious views.

The danger is people pretending to be something they are not, and therefore people need to open and have the courage to share their life, views, and values.

Online dating could be the best tool in the world. However, we must be aware that some people have been hurt, and they don't always act in the best way. You can enjoy the process of online dating when you remove the emotions from it.

Look at it simply as a database of people with whom you can connect and develop relationships. Try not to put many expectations on the outcome of the connection until you have gone off the app.

Your photos are your catalogue to show the best side of you, demonstrating your values and what is important to you.

Having a quality photo is essential; ensure that it is taken with a good camera, lighting, and backdrop. People only have a short period to consider if they want to connect with you, giving yourself the best opportunity for success.

You could invest in professional photos for the apps or upload pictures with friends if you socialize a lot. All these different things show the better side of you. If you're into martial arts, show a picture of yourself doing martial arts.

It's not about pretending to be someone else to attract the right person; it's about being the best version of you to attract the person you want to bring in.

Women's dating app bio:

The key to a female's bio is short and sweet.

Males have short attention spans, and when they come across an extensive bio, it is difficult to digest it.

I love how some of my clients write long essays for the bios, and it's sweet and lovely. However, it doesn't get read, and most importantly, it gives too much away about you. It's like reading a whole book.

We need to keep the suspense up; it's about being short and snappy.

Remember, curiosity killed the cat.

It can open the conversation due to the curiosity and help build excitement getting to know each other. Once you start to connect with a potential partner, you can share your gifts by communicating with them about what is important to you and about your travels.

For example:

Have something about who you are, a quick line such as. I am sweet and funny.

Then write down three things that your friends would describe you as: cute, funny, cheeky, intelligent, courageous, and funny.

These things are important for you to help your potential match see who you are.

Finally, what you want in a partner:
I want a partner that is into Bollywood movies and romantic walks.

I want a partner into personal development and deep, meaningful conversations.

Many clients have used this approach, and it has worked out well to connect with people.

It's essential for you to show the best part of you and for them to be curious enough to be able to understand you and get to know you.

Men's dating app bio:

Guys, many women have said, the more, the better. Remember, a female is ready to read the bio and take their time to understand more about you before they swipe.

I want you to be open and honest about what you want and who you are.

Such as:

I want a family-oriented spiritual woman who can enjoy the finer things in life. I am ambitious, driven, and deeply connected with God and the universe. I have my own business and want to impact the world.

Or

I want a woman I can go to the theatre with while having amazing conversations about the world. I am a man that loves fine wine and has a deep connection with the right woman.

It will allow women to connect with you to understand what you want and be clear on the man you are.

Messaging will always be awkward initially.

Who should message first?

Should guys go first, or women go first?

It doesn't matter as much. It is more important to develop a deeper relationship sooner, which means opening and being vulnerable, expressing yourself, and creating attraction.

Act as if you're talking to a friend, you've not seen in a while.

Males should also ask more questions.

I want you to ask questions and allow the females to open and answer, hear them, and connect to their answers.

Share your experiences and about yourself, continuing the conversation. (Although this seems obvious, many people are not connecting with others and asking for what they want).

Leaders ask questions. Therefore, males connect and ask away, allowing the females to express themselves.

Here's a quick game. I used to play this game when I was single; it's called the 5 Questions.

You have five questions to ask each other, and they cannot be the same question.

By asking questions you wouldn't usually ask, you can get to know them better.

I suggest one question in each of these topics:

Fun
Family
Embarrassing
Adventures
Deep
Playful

It is a great tool to connect and create an interesting conversation while expressing yourself so other people get to know you.

Master the fine line technique:

Making too much
effort and caring
about the outcome

Not caring at all and
playing the numbers
game

**THE SWEET SPOT.
SHOWING YOUR BEST
SIDE AND NOT CARING
ABOUT THE OUTCOME**

Initially, people go on these dating sites and give it their total effort. Then get hurt by someone and take it to heart. Or somebody ignores them, ghosts them, and we know how the story goes.

Now: They stop trying online and do not care; they become the problem.

It now creates more ghosting and a lack of effort in messages. It continues into a vicious cycle, and now everyone's frustrated.

The fine line is when you put enough effort in but do not take things personally as you have met them and formed a relationship; you still show your best side but do not get too excited online.

Remember, I have a fantastic Facebook group for singles to join and share about themselves to connect with others. https://linktr.ee/sunnysekhon

The key to online dating is your state beforehand, and you must manage your mindset.

One of my clients was having a hard time with online dating, and after our first call, she adopted another state before going on online apps. She shortly met her partner and developed a deep relationship together, and they are now living together.

I highly recommend creating the ambiance before going online to connect with your future partner. Listen to some music, relax, create an environment that is fun and uplifting. I know some people who use their dating site while in the toilet; we all know what result that will get them.

Think of other ways that you meet a partner. Can you go to coffee shops, the gym, personal development events, single events?

These options will ensure that you do not burn out from online dating.

Online dating is like Netflix; there are many great programs and movies to pick from that we get spoiled for choice. Before, we only had channels one to five, and we would be happy with that.

It is a quality problem; it means we have more variety. However, it is essential to invest in people you connect with to build deeper relationships.

I highly recommend that when you're getting to know somebody, you get to know more than one person at the start. That way, you have one or two dates, and you can select the partner that you genuinely like.

You can understand what they're like, what their behaviours are, who you like, and who you have the most profound connection with.

Many of my clients struggle with this because they always had a belief. The old idea is that I can only date one person at a time. With this idea, they invest too deep into the relationship, and if it doesn't work, they end up hurt again.

It's time to date, guys; you must be asking women out on dates. It's the guy's that led, to ask the woman on a date, you must step into courage to take the risk, and I'm sure it will pay off. If you get rejected, it's not a problem. Rejection is only a false belief of fear.

When we initially believe we get rejected, it's a scary thing. We start to think we are not good enough for the person. We believe that we cannot attract this partner. It is a false belief that is inaccurate and not a true reflection of what's going on in this person's life.

Most of the time, the person rejects other people because of something they are going through. Otherwise, they will politely decline you. It is an internal issue. Something is happening in their life.

There are several things involved, but we have to look at it from how we've conducted ourselves. Ask yourself: How have I behaved? Have I been funny? Have I been lifting? Have I been creating a connection? And then from there, we can say, ok, have I been an idiot towards this person in this way? It's not worked out so well.

Then fair enough, that's your fault.

If you've connected and you've been able to shine your light and make her laugh and give it your best effort, and there's still no spark, then that's fine. It's time for you to step away. Just remember, it's not a rejection of you.

Remember to stay in your strong, courageous, and joyous state.

Staying secure when you are out on dates means that you are in your Queen or King state, feeling confident and aware of your worth. The minute you get caught up in the avoidant anxious state, the relationship will go downhill.

Staying secure within yourself means if they don't text for a day, or it takes two days, then it's ok. You must keep calm and stay centred.

Know your worth.
Know who you are.

When giving feedback to avoidants, one of the critical things to do is to use the sandwich technique.

The sandwich technique involves complimenting them, then share what you need to discuss and ending the conversation with a compliment, for example:

I am enjoying getting to know you, and I want you to know I would like more effort, phone calls, or texts to help the relationship grow.

We get on well, and I would hate to waste this connection.

It is a powerful technique when connecting with an avoidant individual because they will not feel attacked.

I remember I did this with a client.

The partner she was speaking to put her down; he realized what he was doing wrong and apologized when she used the sandwich technique. They are now married and are on their way to creating a beautiful relationship.

If you meet somebody that's a bit more anxious, and over-messaged and calls too often, it would be best to reassure the person to feel confident.

If you like someone avoidant, you must be clear of what you tolerate and respect their space to grow in the relationship.

Remember: you are more than enough, and you deserve love!!

Chapter 12:

Becoming

*Creating an environment based on your values and traits is
the soil for a healthy relationship to flourish.*

I was in a bar the other day, and someone recognized me
for my work and approached me while he was speaking
with a female.

He tried to put me down with his words and undermined
me with his behaviour. It wasn't an issue for me; however, it
is a massive issue in the world.

When people try to undermine others, it shows massive
insecurity within themselves. They are knocking others
down because they do not believe they are good enough.

It is important to know yourself and this chapter is about
becoming the person you say you are to attract the partner
you want.

Imagine: if you are undermining others to cover up your
insecurity, what type of person would you attract? If they
outdo you, will you undermine them because of your
insecurity?

The reason why these behaviours don't affect me is that I
know who I am. I am growing every day, and I know my

values, and I match this with actions to ensure I am congruent.

When you live who you are every day, it is tough for you to be put down due to someone else's insecurity, especially if you have habits that serve the identity you have created.

We will constantly be tested in life, and sometimes, it will be by a potential partner, a colleague, a friend, or even family. Knowing yourself and being your authentic self will allow you to express how you feel if you felt their interpretation of you was inaccurate.

Who must you be and become to maintain the ideal relationship for the future?

The key is to live what we say through daily actions and habits that reinforce the values you want within a relationship.

Here are a few of the most common values for long-term successful relationships:

Integrity:

Integrity is the backbone of deep, long-term relationships. It is essential to have the integrity to create a lasting relationship as you become the person you say you are.

When you say you are a certain way, having integrity aligns your words with your actions.

To apply it, we need to understand what integrity is. What do you need to do daily to have a life of integrity? Do you need to work out, eat healthily, meditate? Do you need to talk positively about people rather than gossip?

Allow yourself to be confident within your abilities if somebody challenges your integrity. The way I look at it is rather than saying; I'm a man of integrity; I will also support this by my words and actions.

To have integrity, I must be loyal, caring, and treat people around me with respect and kindness, honouring my body and living a healthy lifestyle.

By living a healthy lifestyle, I make it a discipline to fast, eat well, and have two litres of water daily. As simple as it is, my integrity values shaped my life.

Showing up to meet people I make commitments with and sticking to my word is another way I have integrity.

If anyone were to approach me and say, you're not a man of integrity, I can confidently say they are wrong as I live with integrity every day through my actions.

If I connect with somebody and give them my word, I follow through, ensuring that I do what I say, living with integrity.

Ask yourself what does it mean for you to be living with integrity? And then, when you're connecting with your partner, I want you to share your integrity values.

Another way my integrity has grown over the last two years is by caring about the world's humanity and giving back beyond my needs.

Serving and giving to charity, voicing my opinion if it mattered, communicating honestly if I believed something wasn't right, and supporting the world is living in my integrity.

Loyalty:

Loyalty is something that everyone wants within a relationship. We all search for loyalty and a deep connection. We want our partner to be there for us.

What does loyalty mean? Is it supporting somebody you care about, or does it mean that you don't cheat on somebody? Is that being loyal?

My definition of loyalty is having your partner's back, having your friends back, having your family members back, and supporting them when needed. If somebody disrespected one of my friends, I would support them even if it meant I'd be the odd one out.

Having loyalty is essential for me to have with my family and friends. They're the people I give the most love to because they're the ones that mean the most to me.

If you want a loyal partner, you must be loyal as well. Being trustworthy is how you create an environment that attracts somebody who is also the same.

When you create habits that match your values, the subconscious mind will attract people with the same values.

If you gossip about friends, you will attract people that talk about you. These habits create the life you have and your reality.

When connecting with a potential partner, you should state that loyalty is very important. I encourage you to be open. Sharing stories of loyal friends and experiences is how others learn about each other.

Honesty:

Honesty is important within relationships; communicating openly and honestly is a pillar of a beautiful relationship.

There are two types of honesty: immature and mature and understanding the difference is powerful.

Immature honesty is when I say something that I don't like about you, and isn't constructive. It's coming from a selfish place to knock your confidence or put you down.

Mature honesty is having that person's back and wanting the best for them by knowing that when you give them this feedback or advice, you will help their life for the better.

When we're looking at honesty, sometimes communication can get very difficult, where you don't want to say what you truly feel.

You may feel that you're not attracted to somebody, or their actions have put you off. You keep this from them and hide the truth. This is when you become dishonest, and you will attract more of this by being dishonest.

Honesty is going into the nitty-gritty, saying 'I care about you, and I want this relationship to work'. However, not messaging me every day isn't helping the relationship grow. I see potential in this relationship and would like to invest in it more.

Honesty could also look like: 'I'm feeling a bit insecure right now because of some bad feedback at work. Sorry if I am short with you'.

Honest communication helps create confidence and secureness within the relationship, and most importantly, a deeper connection. When I know you're honest, I can trust you more and develop a deeper relationship rather than being annoyed and projecting your insecurities onto others.

This is common when people are getting to know each other. They project fears of the relationship not working on to the other person and find faults within them.

If you practice mature honesty daily, it will strengthen this muscle and attract more honest people into your life.

Passion:

Passion is a beautiful value to have in a relationship as it creates chemistry and excitement.

To create passion within the relationship you must experience passion in your life. The more passion you experience daily, the more it will be created within your relationship.

What excites you, what creates passion within your life? Is it going to the gym? Is it working out? What is it that creates a passion that drives you crazy?

I'm passionate about helping people. I love the joy of helping someone breakthrough to the next level of life!

It truly lights me up, it fills me with joy when a client has success within a relationship, and they are making changes in life.

Take something up that you're going to be passionate about daily, if not daily, at least once a week to get you excited.

Health:

Another key value is health for males and females. It is essential because a part of our brain considers reproduction based on another person's health. Part of the survival brain is continuously looking at what will make me survive for longer.

Therefore, we are naturally more attracted to people that give us a higher chance of reproduction. If you're unhealthy and not working on your health, naturally, this isn't as attractive because the brain in the survival mind is saying it will be difficult to reproduce in the future.

Health is essential for attraction and, most importantly, to have this habit so you can live more of a fulfilling, happy life.

What are your health habits?

Working out?
Eating well?
Drinking two litres of water?

These healthy habits ensure you are becoming healthy even if the scales do not always show it.

Confidence:

Many of us want a confident partner as well as confidence within ourselves. Confidence is a muscle that we need to use. The muscle only grows outside of our comfort zone.

Activities within our comfort zone tend to keep us at the same level of confidence and will deplete our confidence levels.

The best way to build more confidence is expanding your comfort zone, doing things that put you in a position or in a state where you must become more confident. You could go to dating events, dating apps, etc.

Using courage is a great way to have confidence. The more you live with courage, the more your confidence grows.

When looking at confidence, an essential thing for me is what you focus on. Focusing on positive outcomes and taking steps towards them helps create more of the life you want.

A habit for me is doing something that I don't want to do, which pushes me. I use it as a trigger to do it despite my hesitation.

I believe what you resist will persist. Therefore, looking into the areas of life you resist the most will help us grow.

Family orientated:

Being family-oriented is a beautiful value for creating a more profound and lasting relationship. Many people who are family orientated look at this as a number one need for a partner.

The issue commonly comes up when people are family orientated is they do not recognize all that they do for the family and believe it is the norm. Consciously being aware of what we do for our family, the love and support we give them, and showing up with beautiful energy are essential to creating a beautiful family environment.

If you were looking for somebody family orientated, you must share about your values and family. What they mean to you, this will allow them to understand that this person has similar values.

Ambitious:

Ambitious is a solid value that many people desire and want. Being congruent with the value of ambition focuses on growth and learning, studying, setting goals, sharing your goals with potential partners, and taking massive action to achieve them.

Surging is an essential key for a relationship to become more within a relationship and grow in life. Having that ambition and surge mentality means that we can learn, develop and want more.

Listen to a podcast, reading books, watch YouTube videos on personal development, all great things to share with others as they will help attract a partner with similar values.

Like attracts like remember, so other ambitious people meet ambition.

Fun:

Fun is different to many people, simply. You can share funny jokes, tease them or you can even laugh with them to elicit fun and laughter.

If this is something important to you, you can watch more funny videos, share these with a potential partner, or tell jokes.

Kevin Hart makes me laugh, and he is one of the funniest people on the planet. I love how he shares energy, charisma, and carries a beautiful outlook on life.

Listening to Kevin Hart before an evening with friends or when I want to be funnier helps me get into a more fun state.

Caring:

When you show care to others, friends, or family, you must share how you do this. It could be that you make food for the family or help someone out when it is needed.

Sexy:

Sexy is a state which is different for the masculine and feminine energy. Getting into your sexy state before a date or speaking to the opposite sexual energy is essential.

The masculine energy can step into their power, share what they want, have a purpose, and be protective.

The feminine, sexy state has an open personality, sharing their day, allowing the masculine to be decisive and free flowing.

Creating a habit to get into your sexy state will help you to switch off from work and be present within the relationship.

Gratitude:

A habit of gratitude is a magnet to attract the life that you want and to attract an abundant partner; when viewing the world from the lens of lack, you attract more lack when looking at the world from gratitude, it provides more time for you to focus on what's essential in life.

Remember, you are sharing to connect, not to show off.

Final words:

Love is the most profound feeling to have in this life and experiencing it with a soulmate is a true gift. I know that it is possible for you no matter what your circumstances, I have been able to use these strategies and tools to help people that have never experienced love or people that have been truly heart broken and bitter because of the life experiences.

I know that you will create love and raising your consciousness around the area of love will help you attract the love you want.

Specifically based on your previous attachment style, it is essential to have time allocated to relationships, connecting, and developing a meaningful love.

If you were anxious, limit your time and thoughts about a relationship to perhaps an hour, focusing on self-love and yourself.

If you were avoidant, allocate time to focus on a relationship, perhaps an hour a day. Therefore, it means you need to declutter your busy schedule to create room for a relationship to come into your life.

If you were scared: Master working on yourself and taking courageous steps to put yourself out there, sharing the best side of you and all your gifts with others.

If you were secure, you should share how you feel about the other person rather than expecting them to know how you feel.

I'm so grateful and happy that Aron could find a beautiful relationship with the feminine energy. He was able to trust and connect. He overcame his problems with his commitment issues and can now be in a beautiful relationship.

I'm still in contact with him, and he's informed me that there were periods when he felt like running away. But when he remembered that it was secure and ready for a relationship, they discussed issues together. He stepped into the courage to have open conversations and difficult ones to understand his partner. By doing this, they connected at a deeper level.

He said that the most significant changes were becoming a secure attachment style, which helped him attract and step back into that masculine energy but understanding how to connect with the feminine.

Sharon, I'm so over the moon and glad to help her on her journey. She's been able to transform her life, living without any fear. She's opened her heart and recently married a man in the same religion as her with the same background, and they are deeply connected.

Their love is lovely, and it's incredible they got married. She owed it down to the depth of understanding herself and the masculine energy and the letting go process for her at change when she could let go of the past and transmute that energy.

She is in an excellent place with trust, love, and a conscious relationship meeting each other's needs.

Jade has been able to develop deeper relationships now. She's in a long-term relationship. A key takeaway was understanding the keys to a relationship and bringing more spontaneous love and connection to the relationship.

Jade is allowing her femininity to open again. She has let go of the cheating from the past; she has let go of the old story and is in a beautiful, loving relationship where she trusts her partner.

She shows up as her greater self, sets boundaries, and creates magic within her relationship.

I am grateful that you have read this book, and I hope that it will impact you in the same way it has influenced many of my clients to transform their lives.

Remember that you are enough, which means you deserve to have the spectacular relationship you want.

I honestly love you, and I appreciate you. I'm so glad that we are connected now.

I can't wait to hear your success stories!!

Showing up
consistently is the
key to creating a
lasting relationship

Bibliography

Shirzad Chamine - https://www.positiveintelligence.com

https://www.healthline.com/nutrition/10-health-benefits-of-intermittent-fasting

Unlimited Power: The New Science of Personal Achievement Paperback – 2 Jan. 2001 by Tony Robbins

Attached: The New Science of Adult Attachment and How It Can Help You Find--and Keep—Love - Book by Amir Levine and Rachel S. F. Heller

(Tennen & Affleck, 1990; Miller, Smith, Turner, Guijarro, & Hallet, 1996

Joe Vitale, Ihaleakala Hew Len - Zero limits

https://www.researchgate.net/publication/320925193_Posture_and_Social_Problem_Solving_Self-Esteem_and_Optimism - Amy Cudd

Mindset mastery - NLP Luke and Carol

You Are the Placebo: Making Your Mind Matter Paperback – 29 April 2014 by Dr. Joe Dispenza (Author)

Dr Hawkins – Power vs Force

— Alison A. Armstrong, Making Sense of Men

https://www.endviolenceagainstwomen.org.uk/new-data-women-feel-unsafe-at-night/

— Alison A. Armstrong, Making Sense of Men - Book

Intimate Communion Awakening Your Sexual Essence by David Deida

Printed in Great Britain
by Amazon

86682881R00135